consultant editor: Simona Hill

decorative tinware

50 contemporary copper, pewter,
metal foil and brass projects to make

southwater

This edition is published by Southwater

Southwater is an imprint of
Anness Publishing Ltd
Hermes House, 88–89 Blackfriars Road
London SE1 8HA
tel. 020 7401 2077; fax 020 7633 9499
www.southwaterbooks.com; info@anness.com

© Anness Publishing Ltd 2003

This edition distributed in the UK by
The Manning Partnership Ltd
6 The Old Dairy, Melcombe Road
Bath BA2 3LR
tel. 01225 478 444
fax 01225 478 440
sales@manning-partnership.co.uk

This edition distributed in the USA and Canada by
National Book Network
4501 Forbes Boulevard
Suite 200, Lanham, MD 20706
tel. 301 459 3366
fax 301 429 5746
www.nbnbooks.com

This edition distributed in Australia by
Pan Macmillan Australia
Level 18, St Martins Tower
31 Market Street
Sydney, NSW 2000
tel. 01300 135 113
fax 01300 135 103
customer.service@macmillan.com.au

This edition distributed in New Zealand by
The Five Mile Press (NZ) Ltd
PO Box 33–1071 Takapuna
Unit 11/101–11
Glenfield, Auckland 10
tel. (09) 444 4144
fax (09) 444 4518
fivemilenz@xtra.co.nz

A CIP catalogue record for this book is available
from the British Library.

Publisher: Joanna Lorenz
Managing Editor: Helen Sudell
Project Editor: Simona Hill
Photographers and Stylists: Deena Beverley,
Stephanie Donaldson, Rodney Forte,
Michelle Garrett, Janine Hosegood, Rose Jones,
Leean Mackenzie, Lizzie Orme, Debbie Patterson,
Graham Rae, Russel Sadur, Lucinda Symons
and Mark Wood
Designer: Nigel Partridge
Production: Darren Price

Previously published as part of a larger
compendium, *Decorative Tin & Wire*

10 9 8 7 6 5 4 3 2 1

Acknowledgements

The publishers would like to thank the
following people for designing projects
in this book:
Juliet Bawden for the Magic Wand Clock
pp104–105.
Evelyn Bennett for the Photograph
Frame pp48–49, Bird Chimes pp58–60,
Metal Reindeer pp64–65, Jewel Box
pp80–81, Spice Rack pp98–99 and Herb
Container pp118–120.
Penny Boylan for the Embossed
Greetings Cards p21, Lacy Silver Gloves
p22, Musical Scarecrow pp61–63,
Shimmering Temple pp68–69 and String
Dispenser pp94–95.
Marion Elliot for the Moorish Flower
Blind pp38–39, Painted Tin Brooches
pp40–41, Embossed Book Jacket
pp42–43, Painted Mirror pp46–47,
Incense Holder pp52–54, Tin Can
Chandelier pp66–67, Punched Panel
Cabinet pp84–85, Number Plaque
pp88–89 and Regal Coat Rack
pp102–103.
Andrew Gilmore for the Plant Markers
p33, Rocket Candlestick pp50–51,
Metal-faced Drawers pp76–77, Pewter-
look Shelf pp82–83, Chrome Birdbath
pp90–91, Hammered Weathervane
pp100–101, Classic Mailbox
pp112–114 and Lunch Box pp115–117.
Mary Maguire for the Embossed Heart

p20, Treetop Angel pp28–29,
Heart Candle Sconce p36, Metal Mosaic
pp44–45, Fiesta Chandelier pp55–57,
Contemporary Clock pp78–79,
Scrollwork Doorstop pp86–87, Stylish
Suitcase pp96–97 and Mexican Mirror
pp109–111.
Andrew Newton-Cox for Rapunzel's
Tower pp106–107.
Gloria Nicol for the Garden
Candleholders pp24–25, Filigree Candle
Crowns p37 and Copper Birdbath p74.
Michael Savage for the Punched Tin Leaf
Frame pp34–35.
Deborah Schneebeli-Morrell for the
Repoussé Frame p23, Candle Collars
pp26–27, Embossed Birds p30, Tin Can
Insects p31 and Beer-can Candle Sconce
p32.
Judy Smith for the Punched Tin Folk-art
Wall pp92–93.
Stewart Walton for the Cutlery Box p75
and Punched Metal Bucket p108.

Safety note
Working with metal is great fun and
can fill many rewarding hours. For
safety, protective gloves should be
worn when using wire and metal
that has sharp edges.

decorative
tinware

Contents

Introduction

With its shiny, reflective surface, metal is the ideal contemporary decorative material to update your home. You can use metal to make anything from candle sconces, jewellery and picture frames to clocks and birdbaths. Metal foil is easy to manipulate once you have had a little practice, and you will be surprised how the addition of copper, pewter, aluminium and brass will make a difference to your home.

The techniques used include cutting metal and finishing the edges, embossing, punching and soldering. As well as explaining and illustrating all these different techniques, the book contains over 50 step-by-step projects to inspire you to create beautiful metal objects, ranging from a simple embossed heart to a personalized gift, and a more challenging, traditionally styled

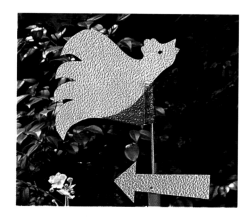

mailbox to attach to your garden gate. The symbol ✂ indicates a project that is relatively straightforward to complete and one which a complete beginner could tackle with ease. Projects with the symbol ✂✂✂✂✂ indicate that an advanced level of

skill and knowledge is required to complete the project. All the materials and equipment required for tinwork can be purchased at hardware stores.

There are plenty of templates included in the book to help you complete the projects; you can trace these or enlarge them on a photocopier to the size required. However, do feel free to adapt these designs or substitute them for your own freehand ideas, if you so desire. When punching or embossing metal, it is worth remembering that simple geometric patterns often work better than complicated patterns, but experimentation is important here. As with all new crafts, practice makes perfect, and this is certainly the case with tinwork. Using the right tools and

equipment is vital, and makes the work far easier to accomplish. When working with metal, safety is important, as cut metal has very sharp edges, so

always wear protective gloves; and, when soldering, remember to wear protective goggles too. Practise first before attempting any of the projects, to get a feel for the metal and its malleability. A steady hand produces the most even indentations and the neatest finish. All practice remnants can be used as decorations for a jewellery box or greetings card, or turned into Christmas tree ornaments.

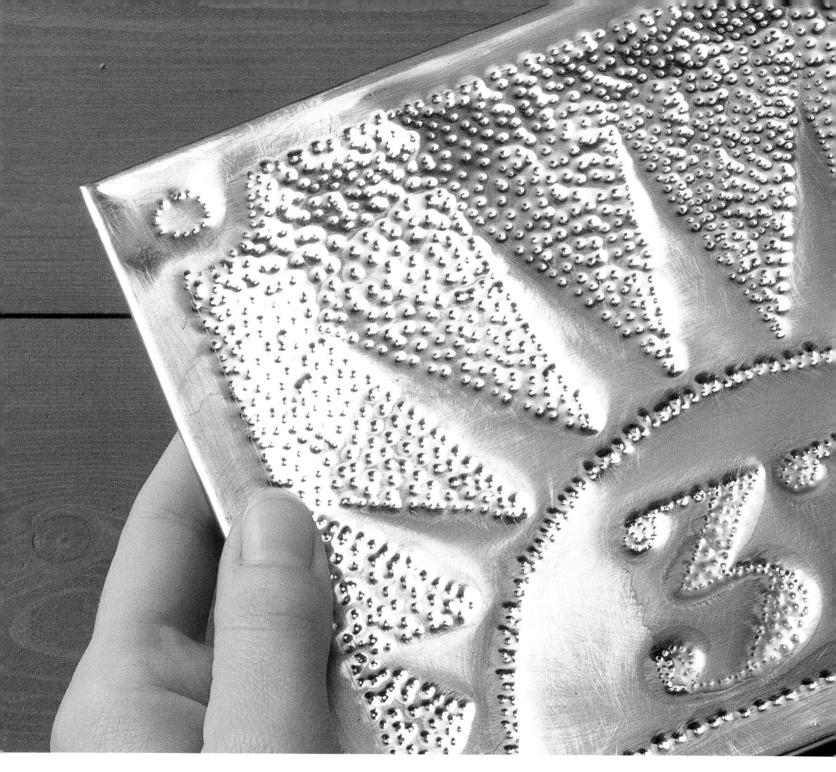

Basic

Techniques

Metal is a material that anyone can use, provided you have the right equipment. The techniques are easily mastered – simply follow the illustrated steps to cutting, embossing, punching and soldering and you will soon be on the road to creating your first metallic masterpiece. Remember that cut metal has very sharp edges so, when working with metal, always wear protective gloves and handle tools with respect.

For tin plate, metal foils and sheet metals, purchase materials from a specialist hardware store, or for recycled materials, a metal merchant or scrap yard. Always wear protective gloves, a work shirt and goggles.

Materials

Silicon carbide (wet & dry) paper
This is abrasive. Fine-grade paper, when dampened, is useful for finishing off filed edges. Clamp the item in a bench vice and wrap the paper around a small wooden block.

S-joiners and jump rings
Use to join sections of an object together and to attach lengths of chain. They are very strong, and pliers are used to open and close the links.

Solder
This is an alloy, or mixture, of metals. Solder is a liquid metal filler that is melted, then used to join two pieces of metal together. Always use a solder that has a lower melting point than the metals to be joined. Follow the manufacturer's instructions.

Tin plate
This is a mild sheet steel that has been coated with tin. The plating will not tarnish in the open air or in humid conditions. Sheet metals are made in different thicknesses, or gauges. The higher the gauge, the thinner the metal. At 30 gauge (approximately 0.2mm/$\frac{1}{125}$in), tin plate can be cut by hand with tin snips and shears.

Biscuit (cookie) tins
A good source of metal. Some have a plastic sheen so scrub with wire (steel) wool, if you intend to solder them.

Epoxy resin glue
This glue comes in two parts. Mix up as much glue as you need at one time. Once it has set the join is strong.

Flux
Used during soldering to make the area to be soldered chemically clean.

As the flux is heated, it runs along the metal preparing the surface. This helps the solder to flow and adhere.

Metal foils
These thin sheet metals usually come on rolls. Metal foil is so thin that it can be cut with household scissors. A variety of metal foils is available, and includes brass, aluminium and copper. The foil's thinness makes it very soft and it is easy to draw designs into the surface.

Zinc sheet
Thin zinc sheet has a dull matt surface and is fairly soft and easy to cut.

You may already have most of the basic tinwork tools. The more specialist items, such as punches, snips and shears, are available from good hardware stores.

Equipment

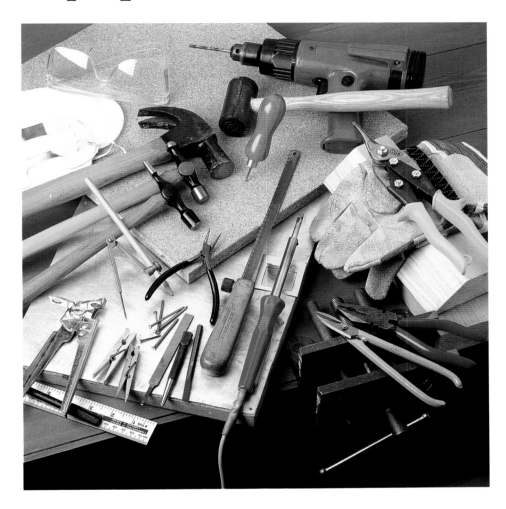

Bench vice
Use to clamp metal shapes when filing, sanding, and hammering edges.

Bradawl (awl)
Use to make holes in metal.

Centre punch, chisel, nails
Use to punch decorative patterns.

Chipboard
This is used as a work surface when punching metal and embossing foil.

Hammers
A variety of hammers are used. A medium-sized ball head hammer is used with nails or a punch to make a pattern in metal. A tack hammer is used to knock panel pins (tacks) into wood. A heavy hammer is used with a chisel to make decorative holes.

Hand file
Use to remove any burrs of metal from the metal after a shape has been cut out.

Hide mallet
This is made from leather. It has a soft head so will not mark the metal.

Pliers
Use to hold metal when you are cutting it and for turning over edges. Round-nosed (snug-nosed) pliers are good for making small circles of wire.

Soldering iron
This is used to heat the solder that joins two pieces of metal together.

Soldering mats
Various fireproof soldering mats are available and may be purchased from good hardware stores and metal supply shops.

Tin shears
These are very strong scissors used for cutting sheet metal. Shears come with straight blades to cut a straight line, or blades curved to the left or right to cut circles and curves.

Tin snips
These are good for cutting small shapes from metal.

Wooden blocks
It is useful to have a wooden block with 90° edges and another with a 45° edge when turning over the sides of a piece of metal.

Only a few basic techniques are required for making simple tinwork items. Read through this section before embarking on the projects in this book.

Techniques

Cutting Metal

It is not difficult to cut through thin sheets of metal plate or cans. It is important to get used to cutting smoothly to avoid making jagged edges, so practise first on scraps of metal. Cutting metal produces small shards of metal that are razor-sharp, so collect scraps as you cut and keep them together until you can dispose of them safely.

Cutting a Section from a Sheet

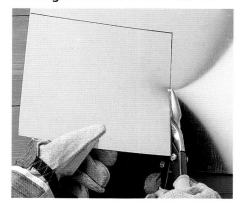

To cut a section of metal from a large sheet, use tin shears. To avoid creating a dangerous jagged edge when cutting, never close the blades of the shears completely. Instead, make a cut almost the length of the blades each time, open the shears, then guide the metal back into the blades and continue. Keep the blades in the cut, without removing them until the line of the cut is complete. If you are cutting a straight-sided shape, don't try to turn the shears around once you have reached a corner. Instead, remove the shears and cut across to the corner from the edge of the sheet of metal.

Cutting a Small Shape from a Section of Metal

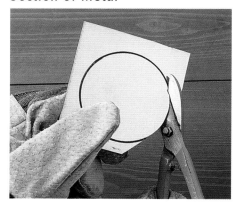

Use tin snips rather than shears to cut small shapes. They are easier to manipulate and control, especially if you are cutting an intricate shape. Again, don't attempt to turn the snips around in the metal; cut as much as you can, then remove the snips and turn the metal so that you can follow the cutting line more easily.

Safety Advice

• Always wear a heavy work shirt and protective leather gloves when you are handling metal pieces or uncut sheet metal.

• Tin shears and snips are very powerful, being strong enough to cut through fairly heavy metal, and very sharp. They should be handled with respect and, like all tools, should always be kept in a safe place away from children.

• A protective face mask and goggles should always be worn during soldering as the hot metal, solder and flux give off fumes. Work should be carried out on a soldering mat and the iron put on a metal rest when not in use.

• All soldering should be carried out in a properly ventilated area and frequent breaks should be taken when working. Don't lean too near your work to avoid close contact with the fumes. Wear protective gloves when you are soldering as the metal is hot.

Cutting Metal from an Oil Drum

1 The metal found in oil drums is very often thin and springy, and so care must be taken when cutting out panels from a drum. Protect your eyes with goggles for extra safety. To remove the top of the drum, make a cut in the side using a hacksaw blade. Open the cut slightly, then insert the blades of a pair of tin shears into the space and cut around the drum, removing the top.

2 Carefully cut down a side to within 18mm/¾in of the drum base using tin shears. Gently snip around the base of the drum, pushing back the panel as it is freed from the base. Once you have removed the panel, it may be used in the same way as a sheet of tin plate. Mop up any oil residue on the surface of the metal using tissue paper.

Finishing the Edges

All metal items should be considered unfinished and unsuitable for use until all the edges have been smoothed or turned over. This should be done immediately to avoid any accidents. Long, straight edges may be folded and flattened with the aid of a hammer and wooden blocks with measured 90° and 45° edges. Irregularly shaped items may be finished with a hand file and silicon carbide (wet and dry) paper for complete smoothness. Tin cans should always be filed smooth around the rims before use to remove any jagged edges.

Filing Cut Metal

The raw, cut edges of a piece of tin plate are very sharp, and should be smoothed or finished immediately to prevent them causing harm to yourself or anyone else. Small shapes should be smoothed with a hand file while being firmly clamped in a vice. The file should be moved forwards at a right angle to the metal in one light stroke, then lifted and returned. This will remove most of the rough edges.

Using Silicon Carbide Paper

To make a cut edge completely smooth after filing, finish with fine-grade silicon carbide (wet and dry) paper. This is dampened and wrapped around a small wooden block like sandpaper (glasspaper). Sanding with this paper removes any remaining rough edges and leaves the metal smooth to the touch.

Turning Over Cut Edges

The cut edges of straight-sided pieces of tin plate should be turned over immediately after cutting to avoid accidents. Mechanically made baking tins and boxes have their edges bent over to an angle of 45° by a folding machine. The edges are then pressed flat and made safe. It is simple to replicate this process at home using two blocks of wood.

1 Clamp a thick block of wood with an accurately measured 90° edge firmly in a bench vice. Draw a border around the cut edges of the tin plate. Place the piece of metal on the block with the borderline lying along the edge of the block. Strike the edge of the metal with a hide hammer to mould around the edge of the block.

2 Turn the piece of metal over and place a block of wood with a 45° edge inside the fold. Keep the wooden block firm with one hand while hammering down on the folded edge of metal with a hide hammer.

3 Once the metal has been folded over to this angle, remove the block then hammer the edge completely flat using a hide hammer. Fold each side of the piece of metal in turn and once all its edges have been hammered flat, file the corners to smooth any sharp edges. Straight edges should always be finished in this way to avoid accidents, even if the panel is to be set into a recess, for example in the case of a punched panel cabinet.

Soldering

Sections of metal may be joined together by soldering. It is essential that both surfaces to be joined are clean before they are soldered. Rubbing both areas with wire (steel) wool will help to remove any dirt and grease. All soldering should be done on a soldering mat, wearing protective gloves, masks and goggles, and the soldering iron should be placed on a metal stand when not in use.

1 Place together the two sections to be joined. Hold them in place with wooden pegs (pins) or masking tape. Smear the joint with flux. This is essential, as when the metal is heated, an oxide forms on the surface that may inhibit the adhesion of the solder. The flux prevents the oxide from forming on the metal.

◀ **2** The hot soldering iron heats the metal, which causes the flux to melt. Pick up a small amount of solder on the end of the iron. It will start to melt. The iron is drawn down the joint and the solder flows with it, and displaces the flux. The solder then cools and solidifies, joining the two pieces of metal together.

Punching Metal

Metal may be decorated in a variety of ways. Punching, when a pattern of indentations is beaten into the surface of the metal, is a common method. A centre punch or nail, plus a ball hammer, are used to produce the knobbly patterns, either on the front or back of the metal. Small chisels and metal stamps are also used. Opaque and translucent enamel paints are suitable for decorating tin plate and other metals. Thin metal foils, such as aluminium foil, are so soft that a design may be drawn on to the surface to leave a raised or "embossed" pattern.

Getting the Design Right

Nails or punches can be used to make indentations and holes in metal. If you want a sophisticated pattern, draw the design first on to a sheet of graph paper and punch through the paper into the metal following the lines. The paper should be taped to the metal, and the metal attached to chipboard using panel pins (tacks) to keep it steady as you punch.

Punching Metal from the Front

A design punched from the front will have an indented pattern. If an area of metal is punched from the front, and the indentations are made very close together, the punched area recedes and the unpunched area becomes slightly raised. This is one form of "chasing", where decorative patterns are punched into metal from the front and stand out in low relief.

Punching Metal from the Back

A design punched from the back will have a raised pattern and a pleasing knobbly effect on the surface. Patterns can be applied with nails of different sizes or punches to make a dotty texture. Short lines can be made by using a small chisel. It is also possible to buy decorative punches with designs engraved into the tip.

Embossing Aluminium Foil ▶

Aluminium foil is very soft thin metal. It can be cut with household scissors and bent or folded as desired. It is especially useful for cladding frames, books, boxes and other small items. Its softness makes it easy to emboss. This is done by drawing on to the back of the foil using a dry or empty ballpoint pen, which leaves a raised surface on the other side.

Right: Many projects combine a range of decorating techniques.

Decorative
Tinwork

Metal is a marvellous material to use in creating decorative items. With its smooth texture, reflective sheen and stark graphic appeal, metal is the new material for the home. A combination of punching, embossing, soldering and mosaic enables you to create jewellery, decorative candle sconces, ornamental picture frames, a Moorish blind and even a musical scarecrow.

Embossed Trinkets

This chapter shows you how to make use of metal in all its guises to create beautiful decorative projects for the home. Starting with easy embossing and simple punching, you can create pretty ornaments and jewellery. Then you can progress on to more complex mosaic and soldering to make chandeliers, incense holders and even a shimmering temple for the garden.

Aluminium and other metal foils are frequently used to create decorative motifs. You can trace or stencil designs on to the metal, then cut out the shapes with scissors. Use foils to make decorations

for greetings cards, ornaments for the Christmas tree and cladding for picture frames. Metal foil is easy to emboss with decorative patterns and motifs. Recycle aluminium drinks (soda) cans to create decorative objects using the

decoration of the can as part of the final pattern. Foil pie dishes and baking tins (pans) make ideal bases for ornaments and have been used in several of the tin projects in this chapter. When making items to hang from the ceiling or a window frame,

use a material that highlights the sheen of the metal, such as metal link chains or gold thread.

An easy way to decorate a metallic surface is to emboss it using a dry ballpoint pen. This creates a raised surface on one side of the metal, rather like

the look of stamped tin, but is easier and quicker to achieve. Traditional punched patterns are made using a centre punch or chisel; you could punch folk art motifs or graphic patterns or create your own designs. Punched metal can be used to decorate picture frames, cupboard doors and even book jackets.

The projects in this chapter are inspired by art from all over the world.

Celtic motifs are used for some of the repeating patterns, while aspects of Islamic art are featured in other items. Vibrant Mexican designs provide the inspiration for some of the bold patterns, while traditional American folk art is used for much of

the decoration of the punched tin projects. Your surroundings will provide other inspiration for creating your own designs.

Make this exquisite embossed heart decoration to personalize a special gift. Metal stencils come in a variety of designs and make embossing foil simple, so this is an easy project to start with.

Embossed Heart

you will need

small, pointed scissors

pewter or aluminium foil, 36 gauge, (0.1mm/^{1}/$_{250}$in thick)

metal stencil

double-sided adhesive tape

self-healing cutting mat

double-ended embossing stylus

sewing needle (optional)

pinking shears (deckle-edged scissors) (optional)

album, box or greetings card

1 Cut a piece of foil large enough to fit the metal stencil plus a small border all around it. Tape the stencil on to the foil, then place on a cutting mat. Use the thin end of the embossing stylus to outline the stencil. Indent the pattern by drawing the outlines, then rubbing over the whole area. Use the thin end of the stylus for small shapes, and the wide end for large areas. For very small shapes, use the blunt end of a needle.

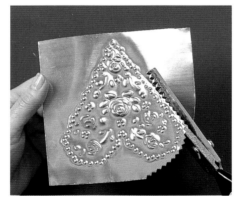

2 Remove the stencil and continue to work on the image to refine it. Cover the indented side of the foil with double-sided adhesive tape, then turn the foil over and cut out the heart shape. For a decorative border, use pinking shears (deckle-edged scissors).

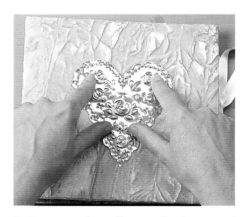

3 Remove the adhesive backing and stick the tin motif on to an album, box or greetings card. To make it even more secure, work the stylus around the edge, pressing in between the raised dots.

Greetings cards decorated with aluminium foil motifs are quick and easy to make. The foil is soft and can be cut with scissors. Designs can be drawn into the back of the foil to make a raised, embossed surface.

Embossed Greetings Cards

you will need

tracing paper

soft pencil

masking tape

aluminium foil, 36 gauge (0.1mm/$\frac{1}{250}$in thick)

thin cardboard

dry ballpoint pen

scissors

thick coloured paper

all-purpose glue

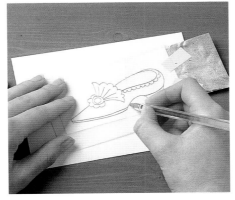

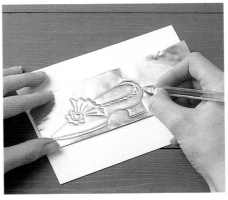

1 Trace the motifs from the templates at the back of the book, then tape the tracing to a piece of aluminium foil and place it on top of a piece of thin cardboard. Carefully draw over the motif with a dry ballpoint pen to transfer it to the foil.

2 Remove the tracing paper from the foil and redraw the lines to make the embossing deeper. Add detail to the design at this stage. Remember any mistakes will show so be sure to follow the markings of your paper template accurately.

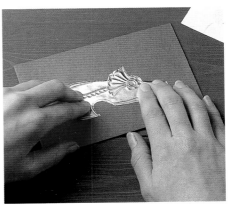

3 Turn the sheet of foil over and cut around the motif, leaving a narrow margin of foil around the outline of the design. Cut a piece of thick coloured paper and fold it in half to make a greetings card. Carefully spread a little glue over the back of the foil motif and stick it to the card, raised side up.

Dainty ladies' gloves make a pretty motif for a traditional glittering tree ornament at Christmas time. Use translucent glass paints to decorate the gloves; they adhere well and let the foil shine through the colour.

Lacy Silver Gloves

you will need

tracing paper

soft pencil

heavy-gauge aluminium foil

masking tape

dry ballpoint pen

scissors

oil-based glass paints

paintbrush

fine gold cord

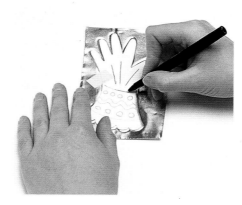

1 Trace the template from the back of the book and attach the tracing to a piece of foil with masking tape. Draw over the design to transfer it to the foil. Remove the tracing and complete the embossing with a ballpoint pen.

2 Cut out the glove, leaving a narrow border of about 2mm/¹⁄₁₃in all around the edge; don't cut into the embossed outline. Carefully make a hole in one corner of the glove with the point of the scissors.

3 Paint the design with glass paints, keeping the colours within the embossed outlines. Allow to dry for at least 24 hours. Thread a loop of fine gold cord through the hole for hanging on the tree.

This delicate foil picture frame demonstrates that repoussé work can be used on objects that are to have a practical, as well as a decorative purpose. Choose foil that is a thicker gauge for such projects.

Repoussé Frame

you will need

tracing paper and pencil

copper foil, 36 gauge
(0.1mm/¹⁄₂₅₀in thick)

adhesive tape

self-healing cutting mat

dry ballpoint pen

ruler

dressmaker's tracing wheel

small, pointed scissors

foam board

double-sided adhesive tape or
all-purpose glue

1 Trace the template from the back of the book. Stick the tracing paper to the copper foil using adhesive tape. Rest the foil on a cutting mat and transfer the design by drawing lightly over the lines with a dry ballpoint pen. Use a ruler for the straight lines.

2 Remove the tracing paper and then use the ballpoint pen to press firmly over the lightly drawn lines. Use an even pressure throughout the whole piece to make the marks consistent.

3 Outline the outer and inner edges using a tracing wheel, then add the crown detail.

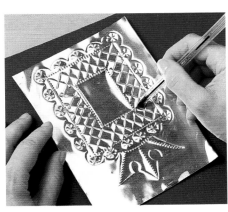

4 Draw the crossed lines. Draw a star in each scallop. Use scissors to cut around the frame. Carefully cut out the centre. Use the template provided to cut out a sheet of foam board. Mount a picture in the centre of the foam board and tape or glue it in place to the board and to the back of the frame. The finished decoration is positioned raised side up.

Plant an instant border of flower candleholders. The materials are easy to find, and are soon transformed into shimmering flower heads, with tall green stems.

Garden Candleholders

you will need

permanent markers

deep-sided foil pie dishes

scissors

stained-glass paints

paintbrush

small foil pie dishes

brightly coloured foil sweet (candy)

wrappers (optional)

epoxy resin glue

night-lights

large flat-headed nails, 2.5cm/1in long

medium green garden canes (stakes)

large foil flan tin (pie pan) (optional)

foil strips (optional)

heavy-duty double-sided adhesive

tape (optional)

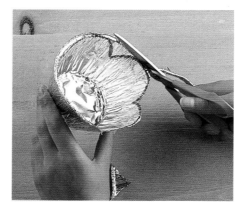

1 Draw the outline of rounded petals on the inside of a foil pie dish with a permanent marker. Cut out the flower shape. Paint the flower, inside and out, with stained-glass paint in a bright, vibrant colour. Leave it to dry thoroughly. Repeat all the above to make more candleholders, painting them in single contrasting colours.

2 Cover a small pie dish with bright sweet (candy) foils if available, smoothing out the foil and wrapping it over the rim to hold it secure. Alternatively, paint with stained-glass paint in a colour that will stand out against the petals already painted.

3 Glue the metal surround from a night-light into the pie dish. Then stick the pie dish inside the flower and push a nail through the centre point of all three layers to hold them together firmly.

4 Push the nail point into the pithy hollow at one end of a garden cane (stake) to fix the assembled flower to it. Add a blob of glue to the joint so it all holds firmly together. When the glue has dried, put the candle into the centre of the flower.

5 If you want to make leaves, mark a large foil flan tin (pie pan) into eight segments with a green permanent marker. Draw curves between the lines along the rim to make heart shapes. Cut out all the segments – each will become an individual leaf.

6 Attach a thin folded strip of foil to the underside of each leaf with heavy-duty double-sided adhesive tape. Paint the leaves on both sides with stained-glass paint. Stick the leaves to the flower stems with another piece of double-sided tape.

These candle collars are based on flower and leaf forms and are embossed from the back in imitation of veining. The beading, though seemingly intricate, is very simple to attach using thin jeweller's wire.

Candle Collars

you will need

tracing paper

soft pencil

thin cardboard

scissors

masking tape

copper foil, 40 gauge
(0.08mm/¹⁄₃₀₀in thick)

sharp pencil

bradawl (awl)

dry ballpoint pen

wooden block

fine jeweller's wire

glass beads

1 Trace the template provided. Enlarge it as required. Transfer it to thin cardboard and cut out. Tape the template to a piece of copper foil. Draw around it using a sharp pencil to transfer the shape to the foil.

2 Remove the template and cut around the outside of the collar. Pierce the centre of the collar using a bradawl (awl). Insert the scissors through the hole and carefully cut out the centre of the collar.

3 Place the collar face down on a sheet of thin cardboard. Redraw over the lines of the outer and inner circles using a dry ballpoint pen. Press a random pattern of dots into the surface of the foil between the two rings. Draw veins on each petal.

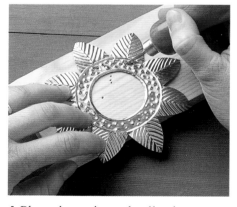

4 Place the embossed collar face up on a block of wood. Carefully pierce a hole directly below the centre of each petal using a bradawl.

5 To attach the beads, thread wire through a hole in the collar, from the back to the front, leaving a short end. Bend the end. Thread a large bead on, then a small bead. Loop the wire over the small bead, thread back through the large bead and up through the next hole at the back of the collar. Attach the beads, cut the wire leaving an end. Twist the ends together.

Adapted from the simple paper angels that we all made as children, this embossed pewter design will add a touch of elegance to the top of your Christmas tree or provide a festive ornament on the mantelpiece.

Treetop Angel

you will need

pencil

paper

masking tape

pewter shim

self-healing cutting mat

dressmaker's tracing wheel

dry ballpoint pen

pinking shears (deckle-edged scissors)

craft knife

permanent marker pen

1 Enlarge the template at the back of the book to the required size. Tape to the pewter shim. Place the sheet on a self-healing cutting mat and use a dressmaker's tracing wheel to trace over the double outlines.

2 Draw over all the solid lines using a dry ballpoint pen. Indent the dots using a pencil.

3 Cut around the shape using pinking shears (deckle-edged scissors). Be very careful when cutting around the halo and wing tips. If you bend some of the zigzag edging, smooth back into shape with your fingers.

4 Turn the angel over. Following the paper pattern, complete the remaining embossed markings from the reverse side, pressing in dots for the eyes and at the centre point of each star.

5 Use a craft knife to cut a slit around the head, inside the halo. Be careful not to cut too near the neck so as not to weaken it. Cut the two slits beside the wings where marked.

6 Roll the head and neck slightly around a cylindrical object such as a marker pen.

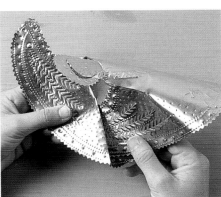

7 Bend the angel's body into a curve and slot together as shown.

Inspired by European folk-art motifs, these foil birds make very pretty ornaments for hanging on the Christmas tree, where their embossed decorations will catch the light as they twirl.

Embossed Birds

you will need
tracing paper
pencil
paper
small, pointed scissors
aluminium foil, 36 gauge
(0.1mm/$^1/_{250}$in thick)
adhesive tape
self-healing cutting mat
dry ballpoint pen
dressmaker's tracing wheel
hole punches, 5mm/$^1/_5$in and 3mm/$^1/_8$in

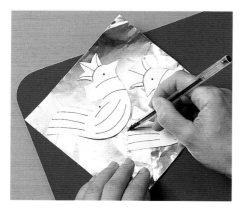

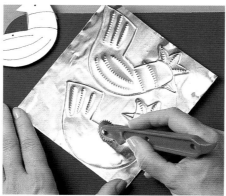

1 Trace and transfer the templates from the back of the book and cut out of paper. Place the templates on the aluminium foil and secure with tape. Place the foil on a cutting mat and draw around the shapes using a dry ballpoint pen.

2 Remove the templates. Draw in the top of the head and the beak of each bird with the ballpoint pen. Use a dressmaker's tracing wheel to mark the dotted lines on the body, tail, neck and crown, following the guidelines on the templates.

3 Draw the eye and the large dots on the wing and neck using the pen. Cut out the birds, cutting just outside the indented outline. Make the hole for the eye with a 5mm/$^1/_5$in hole punch, then use a small punch to make a hole in the bird's back for hanging.

There's more than one way to recycle empty cans: these light-hearted designs turn tin cans into insects to decorate the garden. Use cans with the same logos front and back so that your insects are symmetrical.

Tin Can Insects

you will need

tracing paper

pencil

strong scissors with small points

large aluminium beer can, top and bottom removed

adhesive tape

large paintbrush with a tapered handle

small long-nosed pliers

1 Trace the template from the back of the book and cut it out. Cut up the side of the beer can opposite the bar code and open it out. Place the template in position and secure with adhesive tape. Cut all around the template carefully with sharp scissors.

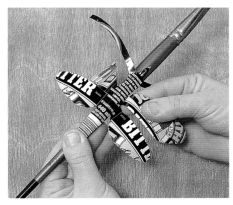

2 Place the body of the insect over the handle of a paintbrush, with the fat part near the head. Bend the body around the handle. Fold the lower wings slightly under the body and the upper wings forwards, folding them slightly over the top of the body.

3 Using long-nosed pliers, twist the antennae back on themselves and curl the ends.

Aluminium cans are easy to recycle into attractive and useful objects such as this candle sconce. The shiny interior of the can makes a most effective reflector for the candle flame.

Beer-can Candle Sconce

you will need

tall aluminium beer can

craft knife

protective gloves

small, pointed scissors

paper

adhesive tape

permanent marker pen

hole punches, 5mm/⅕in and 3mm/⅛in

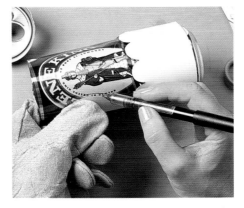

1 To cut off the can top, make a slit in the metal using a craft knife and wearing protective gloves, then cut through the slit with scissors. Enlarge the template at the back of the book to fit your can, and cut it out of paper. Wrap it around the can and secure with adhesive tape. Draw around the shape using a marker pen.

2 Remove the paper template and cut around the design using small, pointed scissors. Make a short slit between each scallop.

3 Use the larger hole punch to make a hanging hole at the top, a hole on either side of the heart shape, and one in each scallop. Use the smaller punch to make a border all round the heart shape. Fold over each punched scallop shape to form a decorative rim for the candle sconce.

These plant markers will lend an air of elegant order to any flower garden. They are simple to construct and will hold together without any glue. Punch the plant name into each marker.

Plant Markers

you will need

tracing paper

soft pencil

thin cardboard

scissors

sheet of copper foil, 36 gauge (0.1mm/$\frac{1}{250}$in thick)

permanent marker pen

sheet of chipboard

bradawl (awl)

pliers

1 Trace the template at the back of the book. Transfer to thin cardboard. Cut out the template and draw around it on the copper foil with a permanent marker pen. Cut the plant marker from the foil using a pair of scissors.

2 Place the copper marker on the cardboard on top of the chipboard. Punch the design and plant name into the front of the marker using a bradawl (awl). Cut all the way up the stem directly under the flowerhead. Using pliers, pleat the middle sections of the plant marker.

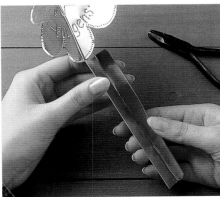

3 Hold the cut strips of the stem together so that the two halves of the bottom petal are joined. Make a fold along the two outer lines of the stem. Wrap the stem around the cut section to hold the marker together.

Tin is a soft metal that can be decorated easily using a centre punch or a blunt chisel to create dots and lines. Keep your punched design graphic and uncluttered as too much fine detail will get lost.

Punched Tin Leaf Frame

you will need

wooden frame

thin cardboard

felt-tipped pen

scissors

adhesive tape

sheet of tin

centre punch

hammer

tin snips

protective gloves (optional)

chisel

ridged paint scraper

copper nails

metal polish & soft cloth (optional)

clear varnish & paintbrush (optional)

paper towels & salt water (optional)

wax & soft cloth (optional)

1 Place the wooden frame on a piece of thin card and draw around the outline with a felt-tipped pen. Add extra length at the outside edges and around the centre to allow for turnings, and cut out the template with scissors. Tape the template on to a sheet of tin. Mark the corners using a centre punch and hammer, and mark the straight lines with a felt-tipped pen.

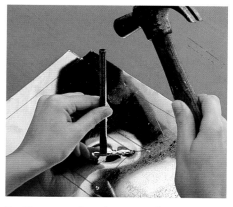

2 Cut out the shape with tin snips. (You may want to wear protective gloves to protect your hands from the tin's sharp edges.) Using a hammer and chisel, cut through the centre of the frame in a diagonal line, then use tin snips to cut along the remaining sides, to leave you with a cut-out square, a little smaller than the centre of the frames.

3 Place the wooden frame on the tin and use a ridged paint scraper to coax the metal up the sides of the frame.

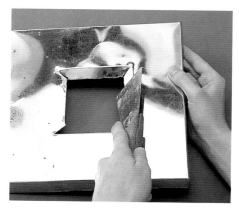

4 Turn the frame over and push down the metal edges in the centre, again using the ridged paint scraper.

5 Cut two strips of tin, each 20cm × 18mm/8 × ¾in. Snip at the halfway mark and fold at a 90° angle. Nail the strips to the inner edge of the frame, using copper nails.

6 Carefully hammer copper nails along the outer edges of the frame so that the tin is firmly secured in place.

7 Draw a freehand leaf design on the tin frame with a felt-tipped pen. Any errors can be easily wiped away. You can vary the design according to your preference for motif, remembering to keep it simple.

8 Press the leaf design on to the tin in dots, using a hammer and centre punch. Alternatively, a blunt chisel and hammer can be used to press the design on to the tin in straight lines.

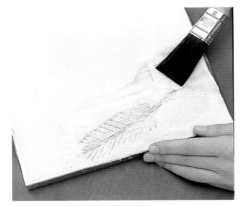

9 There are two ways to finish the frame. Clean the tin with metal polish and a soft cloth, removing any traces of marker pen. To preserve the finish, seal with clear varnish.

10 To rust the tin, cover with a paper towel and dampen with salt water. Keep the paper damp until the frame has rusted – 2–7 days. Remove the paper, leave to dry and seal with wax.

Two small cake tins have been turned into a delightful wall decoration by the clever use of a metal angle bracket. The metal heart will reflect the flickering flame of a small candle or night-light.

Heart Candle Sconce

you will need

6-holed angle bracket

heart-shaped cake tin (pan), 7.5cm/3in

circular cake tin (pan), 7.5cm/3in

permanent marker pen

clamp and masking tape

drill

2 nuts and bolts

spanner (wrench)

wall plugs (plastic anchors)

screwdriver and screw

candle or night-light

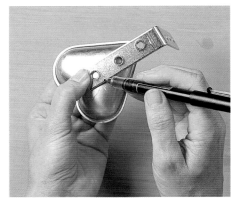

1 Place the angle bracket against the back of the heart tin (pan) and one edge of the circle tin. Mark through the holes in the bracket with a pen.

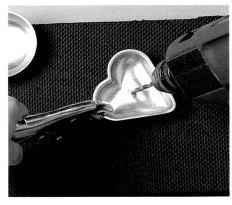

2 Drill through the marked holes. The photograph is styled for clarity – the drill would be perpendicular to the taped and clamped tin.

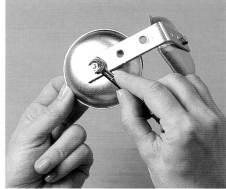

3 Use nuts and bolts to join the round tin to the bracket. Pre-drill and plug the wall, and then screw through the hole in the heart and the bracket into the wall behind. Add the candle to complete the project.

Metallic candle crowns surround and protect the flames and make pinprick patterns of light through punched holes as the candles burn down inside them.

Filigree Candle Crowns

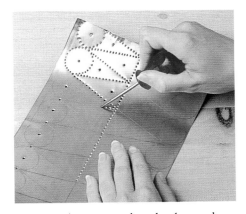

1 Use a sharp pencil and ruler to draw a line across the length of the foil, dividing it in half. Draw diagonal lines across the width of the foil to make a lattice, then draw circles between the parallel lines along the top and bottom edges, using a coin. Protect the work surface with a pile of newspapers. Punch regularly spaced holes along the lines with a bradawl (awl). Punch a hole in the centre of each circle and triangle.

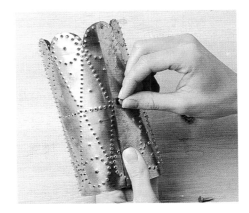

◄ **2** Cut along the top edge with scissors to leave a small border around the punched holes and make a scalloped rim. Bend the foil so that the ends overlap, to form a cylindrical candle crown. Punch through both pieces of foil three times at the overlap. Push a paper fastener through each set of holes to hold the foil in place. Open out the clip ends inside the crown.

This lightweight blind is constructed from bold floral shapes and has a geometric precision that is reminiscent of Islamic decorative motifs. It is easy to hang and can be made to fit any size of window.

Moorish Flower Blind

you will need

protective gloves

scissors

heavy-duty aluminium foil pie dishes

paper

pencil

scrap wood

bradawl (awl)

round-nosed (snug-nosed) pliers

jewellery jump rings (wires)

1 Wearing protective gloves, cut the rim from a heavy-duty aluminium foil pie dish. Enlarge the template to the same diameter as the foil disc. Cut it out, then centre it on the disc and trace around it. Cut out the shape. Make as many as you need for your blind design.

2 Cut some of the flowers in half to make straight-sided pieces for the edges of the blind. Cut one flower shape into quarters to form the four corners of the blind.

3 Arrange the flowers on a piece of wood. Using a bradawl (awl), pierce a hole about 3mm/⅛in from the end of each strut between the flower petals.

4 Using round-nosed (snug-nosed) pliers, open as many jump rings (wires) as you need to join the flowers. Hook a ring through the hole in one strut, and join to an adjacent flower. Close the ring. Repeat with all the flower shapes.

5 Add the side and corner pieces to complete the blind. Add a row of jump rings along the top of the blind from which to hang it.

A good way to use up small scraps of tin is to make brooches. These can be simple in construction and made special with some painted decoration. Enamel paints are opaque and look stunning.

Painted Tin Brooches

you will need

scrap of tin, 30 gauge (0.3mm/¹⁄₈₃in thick)

permanent marker pen

work shirt and protective gloves

tin snips

bench vice

file

silicon carbide (wet and dry) paper

chinagraph pencil

enamel paints

fine paintbrushes

clear gloss polyurethane varnish

epoxy resin glue

brooch fastener

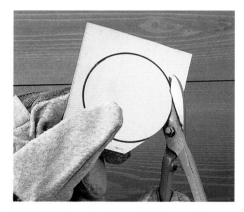

1 To make the brooch front, draw a circle 5cm/2in in diameter on a piece of tin with a marker pen. Wearing a protective shirt and gloves, cut out the circle using tin snips.

2 Clamp the tin circle in a bench vice and file the edges. Finish off the edges with damp silicon carbide (wet and dry) paper so that they are smooth.

3 Draw your choice of motif on to one side of the brooch using a chinagraph pencil. Paint around the outline with enamel paint, then fill in the design. Leave the brooch to dry thoroughly.

4 Paint in the background, then add any features on top of the first coat of paint. Use a fine paintbrush and enamel paint. Leave to dry. Seal the surface with two coats of clear gloss polyurethane varnish. Leave to dry thoroughly between coats.

5 Mix some epoxy resin glue and use it to stick a brooch fastener on to the back. Let the glue dry thoroughly before wearing the brooch.

The appearance of a special book can be dramatically enhanced with an embossed metal panel. The panel covering this book imitates the ornate leather and metal bindings adorning early prayer books.

Embossed Book Jacket

you will need

sheet of aluminium foil, 36 gauge
(0.1mm/$\frac{1}{250}$in thick)

scissors

soft marker pen

ruler

dry ballpoint pen

pencil

thin cardboard

fine paintbrush

gold lacquer paint

epoxy resin glue

1 Cut a piece of aluminium foil the same size as the front of the book. Using a marker pen and a ruler, draw a 6mm/$\frac{1}{4}$in border all the way around the edge of the foil. Divide the area within the border into squares. Draw over the lines to emboss the foil using a dry ballpoint pen. This is the back of the design.

2 Make a cardboard rectangle and circle template. Make them small enough to fit into the grid. Make another circle and rectangle, slightly smaller. Cut out the shapes. Place the large circle in the centre of the first square. Draw around it using a dry ballpoint pen. Repeat with the large rectangle in the next square. Repeat over the whole jacket.

3 Place the small circle inside an embossed circle and draw around it. Place the small rectangle inside a large rectangle and emboss all the shapes in the same way.

4 Draw small double circles and also double semi-circles in each circle. Draw a double oval and radiating lines inside each rectangle. Emboss a dotted line around each rectangle and around the edge of the jacket.

5 Turn the foil over so that it is right side up. Using a fine brush, highlight small areas of the design with the gold lacquer paint. When it is dry, glue the jacket to the front of the book.

Barquette and petit four tins come in delicate, fluted shapes that are too pretty just to bake with. Using them in a mosaic will make you look at them in a new light and make an attractive decoration.

Metal Mosaic

you will need
8 barquette tins, 6cm/2½in long
fluted petit four tin, 3cm/1¼in diameter
biscuit (cookie) tin lid
spatula or small trowel
ready-mixed tile adhesive
diamond-shaped and circular mirror mosaic pieces
cloth or cotton buds (swabs)
strong glue
coloured glass pebble

1 Arrange small barquette and petit four tins inside the lid of a biscuit (cookie) tin until you have a design.

2 Remove the small tins and use a spatula or small trowel to spread an even layer of tile adhesive in the lid. Press the tins into place. Leave to dry.

3 Add a second layer of tile adhesive, filling the lid to the level of the tin rims, and smooth the surface (it may help to wet the surface slightly).

4 While the adhesive is still soft, press mirror mosaic pieces all round the edge of the piece to make a decorative border. Then add small circular mirror pieces between each of the flower petals to complete the mosaic.

5 Wipe the surfaces clean with a damp cloth or damp cotton buds (swabs). Leave to harden. Glue a coloured glass pebble into the tin in the centre to add focus to the design.

Painted tinware is a popular art form in many countries, particularly India and those of Latin America, where fine-gauge tin is stamped with decorative patterns and often highlighted with translucent paints.

Painted Mirror

you will need

sheet of tin plate, 30 gauge
(0.3mm/¹⁄₈₃in thick)

marker pen

ruler

work shirt and protective
leather gloves

tin shears

90° and 45° wooden blocks

bench vice

hide hammer

file

graph paper

scissors

saucer

pencil

masking tape

sheet of chipboard

panel pins (tacks)

tack hammer

centre punch

ball hammer

chinagraph pencil

soft cloth

translucent paints

paintbrush

square mirror tile

aluminium foil, 36 gauge
(0.1mm/¹⁄₂₅₀in thick)

epoxy resin glue

copper foil, 40 gauge
(0.08mm/¹⁄₃₀₀in)

D-ring hanger

1 To make the frame, draw a 30cm/ 12in square on a sheet of tin. Draw a 1cm/²⁄₅in border inside the square. Measure 2cm/⁴⁄₅in from the outer corners along each side. Connect these points by drawing diagonal lines, as shown. Wearing protective clothes, cut out the square with tin shears. Cut along the diagonal lines.

2 Firmly clamp the 90° block of wood in a bench vice. Place the mirror frame on the wooden block with the ruled edge of the tin square resting on the edge. Using a hide hammer, tap along the edge of the tin to turn it over to an angle of 90°.

3 Turn the frame over. Hold the 45° block of wood inside the turned edge and hammer the edge over. Remove the block and hammer the edge flat. File the corners of the mirror frame to remove any sharp edges. Cut a piece of graph paper the same size as the frame.

4 Draw the decorative corner lines on to the paper, drawing around the saucer. Draw the centre square slightly larger than the mirror tile. Tape the pattern to the back of the frame, place it face down on the chipboard and secure with panel pins (tacks).

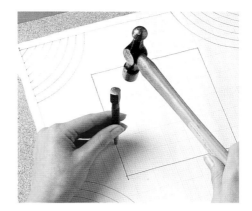

5 Place the point of the centre punch on a line of the inside square and tap it with the ball hammer to make an indentation. Move the punch about 3mm/⅛in along the line and tap it to make the next mark. Continue punching along all the lines until the design is completed.

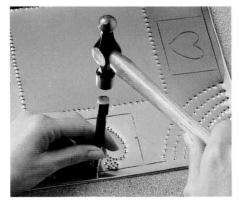

6 Unpin the frame from the board and remove the pattern. Turn the frame over, so the raised side faces up. Using a chinagraph pencil, draw a square halfway along each side. Draw a heart in each square. Pin the frame to the board again and punch an outline around each square and heart. Punch the area between the heart and the square to make a densely pitted surface. Remove the frame from the board. Wipe over the surface of the metal with a clean, soft cloth to remove any grease.

7 Paint the embossed areas and the border. Leave to dry and apply a second coat if the first is patchy. Place the mirror tile on aluminium foil and draw around it, then draw a 1.5cm/⅗in border around that. Cut out the foil. Clip the corners to make folding the edges over easier. Glue the mirror to the centre of the foil. Glue the edges of the foil over the tile.

8 Cut four small squares of copper foil, mark your choice of design on each, then glue one square in each corner of the tile. Glue the mirror to the centre of the frame. Glue the hanger to the back of the frame. Allow the glue to dry thoroughly.

Because of its softness, fine-gauge aluminium foil is just perfect for cladding frames. Coloured and clear glass nuggets combine with the subdued tones of the foil to give this frame a Celtic air.

Photograph Frame

you will need

photograph frame

ruler

aluminium foil, 36 gauge
(0.1mm/¹⁄₂₅₀in thick)

scissors

epoxy resin glue

pencil

thin cardboard

marker pen

dry ballpoint pen

coloured and clear glass nuggets

1 Carefully remove the glass and the backing from the frame. Cut foil strips to cover. Make the foil long enough to wrap around to the back of the frame. Mould the foil strips around and glue them in place.

2 Cut pieces of foil to cover the four corners. Mould to the contours of the frame and glue them in place.

3 Draw a circle on to cardboard and cut out to make a template. Draw around the cardboard on to the foil using a marker pen. Cut out the foil circles. Draw a design on to one side of each circle using a dry ballpoint pen. This is now the back of the circle.

4 Turn the foil circles over so that the raised side of the embossing is face up. Glue coloured glass nuggets to the centre fronts of half of the foil circles. Glue clear glass nuggets to the centres of the other half.

5 Glue the foil circles around the frame, spacing them evenly. Alternate the circles so a coloured glass centre follows one with clear glass. When the glue is thoroughly dry, replace the glass and backing in the frame.

This aluminium candlestick has a cartoon-like appearance that is very appealing. The small sections are constructed first and then joined together. Each section is attached to the next using pop rivets.

Rocket Candlestick

you will need

tracing paper

soft pencil

thin cardboard

glue

scissors

thin aluminium sheet

work shirt and protective

leather gloves

tin snips

file

drill

pliers

90° wooden block

hammer

pop riveter and rivets

black oven-hardening clay

epoxy resin glue

1 Trace the rocket templates from the back of the book. Enlarge the pieces if required using a photocopier. Stick the tracings on to thin cardboard, allow to dry, then accurately cut out each shape.

3 Mark the drilling points on each piece and drill the holes. Hold the metal with a pair of pliers to stop it spinning around while you drill.

2 Cut out the templates and draw around them on to the aluminium. Draw six side sections, three fins and one top shelf. Wearing protective clothes, cut out all the pieces using tin snips and file the edges smooth.

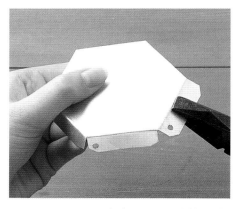

4 Using a pair of pliers, carefully fold down all the sides of the top shelf to make an angle of 90°. Bend the metal over a right-angled object.

◄ **5** Place the side sections on the edge of the wooden block and hammer over the edges. Hold each section and gently curve it outwards.

6 Hold two side sections together with the tabs to the inside. Join the sections with pop rivets at the middle and the bottom holes. Join two more pairs.

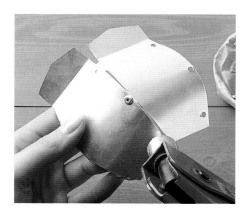

7 Place a fin between two separate side pairs and pop rivet all three layers together at the middle and bottom holes. Pop rivet the remaining side pairs together, with a fin in-between.

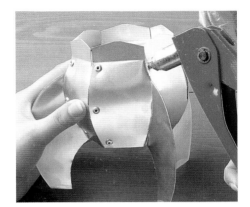

8 Position the shelf at the top of the candlestick with the sides pointing downwards. Join the shelf to the base with pop rivets through the top holes.

9 To make the feet, roll three balls of black clay. Flatten the base of each and make an indentation in the ball top. Bake the clay according to the manufacturer's instructions. When cool, glue a foot to each fin.

This ornate incense holder is reminiscent of ecclesiastical censers, which are used in religious services and processions. Here, two colours of metal foil are heavily embossed and used to encase a humble tin can.

Incense Holder

you will need

can opener

small tin can

file

aluminium foil, 36 gauge (0.1mm/¹⁄₂₅₀in thick)

scissors

pencil

graph paper

masking tape

thin cardboard

dry ballpoint pen

copper foil, 40 gauge (0.08mm/¹⁄₃₀₀in thick)

epoxy resin glue

wooden pole

bench vice

bradawl (awl)

thin metal chain

wire cutters

3 chain triangles

pliers

key ring

glass droplets and nuggets

cardboard tube

metal bottle cap

1 Using a can opener, remove one end of the tin can. Carefully file around the inside top edge of the can to remove any rough edges. To make the covering for the can, cut a rectangle of aluminium foil as wide as the can, and long enough to fit around it with 1cm/²⁄₅in to spare.

2 Draw a repeating design on graph paper to fit the rectangle. Cut it out. Tape the aluminium foil to a sheet of cardboard, then tape the pattern over the top and draw over the lines using a dry ballpoint pen. Press hard so the pattern will be embossed on the foil.

3 Cut a shorter, narrower rectangle of aluminium foil for the lower section. Draw out the decorative pattern for this section on to graph paper. Cut out the paper pattern and transfer it to the narrower strip of aluminium foil as before, using a dry ballpoint pen.

4 Draw a flower on thin cardboard and cut it out to make a template. Transfer the template to copper foil and cut out. Cut as many flowers as you need to fit around the can. Place the flowers on thin cardboard and draw decoration on to the petals.

▶

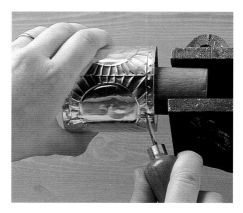

5 Glue the covering around the can using epoxy resin glue. When the glue is dry, firmly clamp a short length of wooden pole in a bench vice. Rest the can on the pole and make three holes at equal distances in the top edge using a bradawl (awl).

6 Cut three lengths of chain, each 12.5cm/5in. Fix a chain triangle through each hole in the top of the can and, using pliers, attach a length of chain to each. Attach the other ends of the chains to a key ring.

7 Make six evenly spaced holes along the bottom edge of the lower section of the burner using a bradawl. Carefully attach a small glass droplet to each hole, alternating the colours, and tightening the wires of the droplets with pliers.

8 Clip tabs along the top edge of the lower section of the aluminium foil. Wrap around a cardboard tube and glue the edges together. Leave to dry and remove from the tube. Bend out the tabs and glue to the underside of the can.

9 Glue the copper flowers around the can with their raised surfaces facing outwards. Glue a glass nugget in the centre of each flower, alternating the colours of the nuggets.

10 To make a holder for the incense cone, glue a metal bottle cap to the inside centre of the can.

This flamboyant chandelier has been created using baking accessories and tins, which come in a wide range of interesting shapes and sizes to inspire you.

Fiesta Chandelier

you will need

fluted flan ring, 30cm/12in diameter, 2.5cm/1in deep

permanent marker pen

galvanized wire

wire cutters

round-nosed (snug-nosed) pliers

blue glass paint

paintbrush

permanent felt-tipped pens: turquoise, green, orange, yellow and pink

9 fluted petit four tins

self-healing cutting mat

hammer

galvanized nails, 2.5cm/1in long

centre punch (optional)

paper

pencil

scissors

aluminium sheet

protective gloves

tin snips

chisel-ended bradawl (awl)

brass paper fasteners

strong glue

glass nuggets

3 wired glass bead necklaces or plug chains

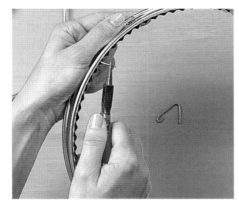

1 Count the flutings on the inner flan ring and mark off three equal sections. Cut three short pieces of wire and then thread them through the fluting at the marked points. Make a loop at the top of each wire using pliers and bend the other end up inside the fluting to secure the loop.

4 Place the petit four tins on a self-healing cutting mat and use a hammer and nail or centre punch to drive a hole through the centre of each tin. Colour the outside of the tins orange with a felt-tipped pen.

2 Paint the inside of the ring, and the wire loops, with blue glass paint. Leave to dry.

3 Colour the outside of the ring with turquoise and green permanent felt-tipped pens.

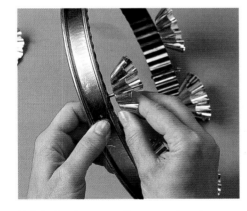

5 Mark nine equally spaced points on the ring for the candleholders. Press a nail through the centre of each of the petit four tins and insert in the flutes of the ring.

▶

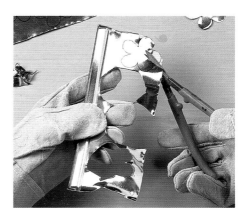

6 Draw a flower 5cm/2in in diameter on paper and use this template to draw nine flowers on the aluminium sheet. Cut out using tin snips and wearing protective gloves.

7 Cut one aluminium flower twice the size of the others for the crown at the top of the chandelier. Colour all the flowers using felt-tipped pens.

8 Using a chisel-ended bradawl (awl), cut a slit in the centre of each of the aluminium flowers.

9 Slot a brass paper fastener through the centre of each coloured flower. (Check the size of an opened fastener against the depth of the flan ring – you may need to trim the tips.)

10 Fix on the flowers by sliding the open tips of the paper fasteners under the rolled rims of the flan ring in between the candleholders. Add a spot of strong glue to hold securely. Glue the glass nuggets to the ring midway between the flowers.

11 Thread a length of wire through the large flower and bend it into a hanging loop at the top and a hook beneath the flower. Attach three necklaces or chains to the loops on the ring and suspend them from the hook under the flower.

This wonderfully eccentric four-legged bird floats in the air and the passing breeze moves its chiming legs. Its body is a tin can and thin tin plate has been used to make its wings, head and tail.

Bird Chimes

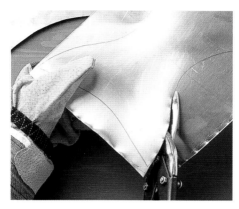

1 Remove both ends of the tin can. File the inside of each rim to remove the rough edges. Trace the templates from the back of the book, enlarging them as necessary, and transfer them to thin cardboard. Cut out. Place on the tin plate and draw around them. Wearing protective clothes, cut out all the shapes using tin shears. File each piece to remove the rough edges.

2 Curve each head and tail section inside the tin can. Hold them in place on the tin using wooden pegs (pins). Place the tin can on a soldering mat and, wearing a protective mask and goggles, apply flux and solder along the joins. Curve the two halves of the bird's head together and keep them in place with wooden pegs. Solder along the join. When the metal is cool, file around the beak.

3 Using tin shears, cut the underside of the body. Leave a gap of about 2cm/⅘in between the two curves at the narrowest point, for hanging the legs. File the edges smooth.

4 Using a hammer and nail, punch two holes near the edge of each side of the body for the legs, and one in the top for the hanger. File the rough edges. Attach the wings with masking tape, then solder.

▶

5 Using pliers, turn the unscalloped edges of the wings over and squeeze them flat. Carefully file away any remaining rough edges on the wings, then repeat this process to finish the tail.

6 To make the legs, cut four lengths of copper tubing each 20cm/8in using a hacksaw. Cut each piece in half again and file away the rough edges.

7 Wrap strips of masking tape around the ends of the tubing. Clamp the tubing and drill a hole in each end. The tape will stop the drill bit from slipping. Join both halves of each leg together using lengths of fine wire.

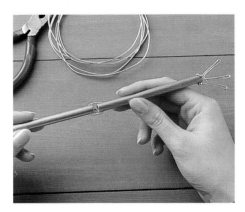

8 Cut four lengths of fine wire and use pliers to shape each piece into a foot. To join the feet to the bird's legs, push the ends of each foot into the holes in the end of the legs and apply a dot of solder.

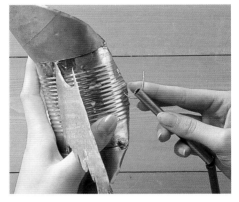

9 Pass a length of wire through one of the holes in the side of the bird's body. Attach a leg to the wire and twist the ends together to keep it in place. Attach the other three legs to the bird's body in the same way. Using pliers, make a hook from fine wire and push it through the hole in the top of the bird's body. Bend the wire to hold it in place. Attach a split ring to the hook to make a hanger.

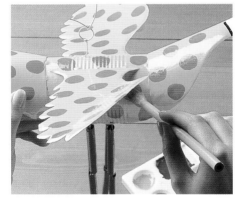

10 Apply one coat of metal primer to the bird, leave to dry, then apply a coat of bright yellow enamel paint. When the paint has dried, add orange dots. Paint all the legs red and the feet black. Use black, white and blue paint to add detail to the tail and head.

This scarecrow will bring a note of whimsy to your vegetable garden, and she will also protect your crops from marauding birds by rattling and jingling in the breeze.

Musical Scarecrow

you will need

assorted aluminium drinks (soda) cans

scissors

tracing paper

pencil

adhesive tape

ruler or tape measure

madeleine mould

centre punch

hammer

brass paper fasteners

galvanized wire

wire cutters

pliers

6 copper pipe connectors, 15mm/⅗in wide

rectangular can

fine wire

1 Using scissors, cut off the tops and bottoms of the cans. Cut along the side seams and open them out flat. Trace the templates from the back of the book and cut them out. Attach to the metal sheets with adhesive tape and cut around the shapes. Reverse one hand and one shoe to make pairs. Cut out a small flower shape for the scarecrow's knees.

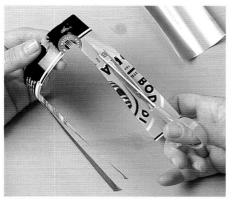

2 For the scarecrow's hair, cut a long rectangle from a can to the same width and twice as long as the top section of the madeleine mould. Cut out the centre of the rectangle, leaving a 2cm/⅗in strip at the top and down each side. Cut each side piece into two strips, as shown.

3 Curl each long side strip around a pencil. Make three holes around the top edge of the madeleine mould with a centre punch and hammer.

4 Fasten the hair to the madeleine mould using paper fasteners. Pierce a hole in the foot of the mould and thread with a short galvanized wire loop, which will fasten the head to the body.

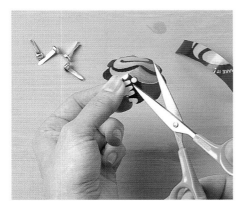

5 For the bikini top, cut a slit to the centre of each flower. Bend into a cone and fix by piercing both layers with the scissors and inserting a paper fastener. Thread the fastener ends through the strip to join the top. ▶

6 Make the fringed skirt by cutting a rectangle of metal into a fringe. Cut a strip for the belt and cut a buckle shape in a contrasting colour. Slot the belt through the buckle.

7 Make the arms and legs by rolling up six rectangles of can. Slot each one through a 15mm/⅗in copper pipe connector to keep it rolled up.

8 Cut four lengths of galvanized wire slightly longer than the arms and legs and make a hook in one end. Pierce the hands and the feet and thread one of the hooks through each hole. Twist with pliers. Slide a tube on to each wire and then bend the straight end of the wire into a loop.

9 Use a centre punch to make one hole in each side and two holes in the base of the rectangular can, which will form the body. Thread a length of wire through the two shoulder holes, so that it protrudes from each side. Thread each end into the loops at the top of the arms, then bend into a loop and twist to secure. Cut off the excess.

10 Fold another length of wire in half and thread through the body so it protrudes through the holes in the base. Thread the last two tubes on to these, then thread the wire through the loops on each lower leg section. Twist the wire to secure it and trim away any excess.

11 Pierce the kneecap flowers with a paper fastener and secure through the wire loop on each leg. Using fine wire, attach the clothing and fix the body to the wire loop on the head.

This charming reindeer is made from zinc plate that is thin enough to curve and manipulate easily. Zinc plate is steel that has been coated with a thin layer of zinc to protect it from corrosion.

Metal Reindeer

you will need

tracing paper

soft pencil

thin cardboard

scissors

thin zinc plate

marker pen

work shirt and protective
leather gloves

tin snips

file

paintbrushes

small hammer

soldering mat

flux

protective mask and goggles

soldering iron and solder

masking tape

fine wire

wire cutters

pliers

enamel paints: red, blue, yellow
and black

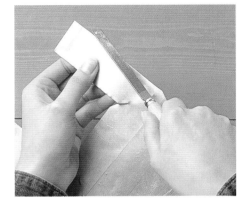

1 Trace the head and body from the back of the book, enlarging them if necessary. Transfer to thin cardboard and cut out. Draw around each on to a sheet of thin zinc plate using a marker pen. Wearing protective clothes, cut out the head and body using tin snips. File all the edges smooth. Draw and cut out two ears.

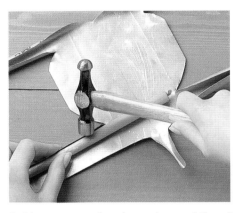

2 Place a paintbrush in the middle of each leg and the tail and gently tap the metal with a small hammer to curve it into a cylinder. Curve the reindeer's body. The reindeer will now stand upright. Place the reindeer on a soldering mat and apply flux to the joins. Wearing a protective mask and goggles, spot solder along the inside of each leg and the body.

3 Gently curve the reindeer's neck to make a cylinder. Hold the edges together with masking tape while you spot solder along the join. Gently bend the head downwards and curve the sides to make it cylindrical.

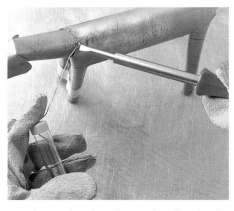

4 Place the head inside the body. Wrap a strip of tape around the front legs to pull tightly together so that the head fits snugly inside the body section. Solder along the join where the neck meets the body.

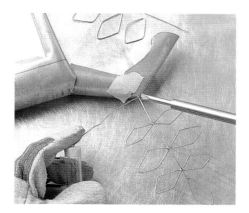

5 To make the antlers, cut two long and 14 short pieces of wire. Bend the short pieces into diamonds, and then solder to the two long pieces. Tape the antlers to the head and solder.

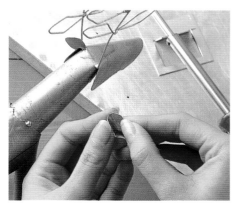

6 Curve the ears, tape in place and solder them next to the antlers.

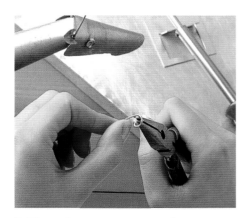

7 To make eyes, cut two short pieces of wire and twist around the end of the pliers to make spirals. Solder the eyes to the sides of the head.

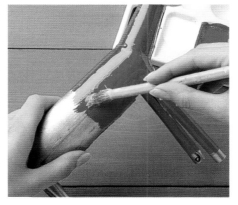

8 Paint the reindeer, except for its antlers, with two coats of red enamel paint, allowing the first coat to dry before adding the second.

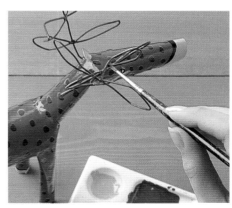

9 When the red paint is dry, paint blue spots on the body. Paint its ears, hooves and nose yellow. Paint a black line around the nose and the hooves and paint the antlers blue.

This chandelier is made from eight small tin cans and a tin flan ring. The chandelier is suspended from strong beaded chain; buy the kind with forged links that can withstand the weight of the chandelier.

Tin Can Chandelier

you will need

tape measure

marker pen

tin flan ring, 30cm/12in in diameter

wooden block

bradawl (awl)

file

can opener

8 small cans

length of wooden pole

bench vice

8 nuts and short bolts

screwdriver

pliers

4 S-joiners

strong beaded chain

wire cutters

4 jump rings (wires)

key ring

epoxy resin glue

coloured glass nuggets

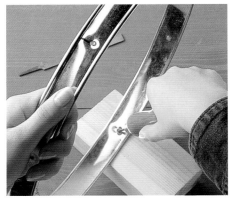

1 Measure and mark eight evenly spaced points around the flan ring. Rest the ring on a block of wood and pierce a hole at each point using a bradawl (awl). File away the rough edges at the back of the holes.

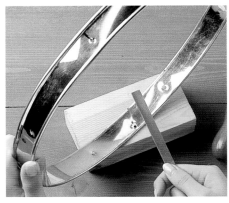

2 Mark three equally spaced points near the top edge of the ring. These holes will be used to suspend the chandelier from the beaded chain for hanging. Pierce them with a bradawl as before and file away the rough edges.

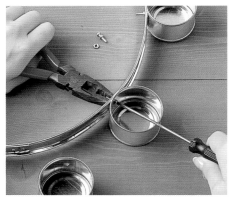

4 Place each can against a hole in the flan ring. Join the cans to the ring using short bolts. Screw the nuts on to the bolts as tightly as they will go so the cans are kept firmly in position.

5 Attach an S-joiner through each of the three holes in the top of the flan ring. Using pliers, close the joiners as tightly as they will go.

3 Remove the top from each can and file the edges smooth. Mark a point halfway down each can (avoiding the seam). Clamp a length of wooden pole in a bench vice. Support each can on the pole and pierce a hole in the side at the marked point using a bradawl. File any rough edges at the back of the holes.

6 Cut three lengths of beaded chain each 30cm/12in. Attach a jump ring (wire) to the end of each length of chain. Attach a length to each S-joiner. Tightly close the jump rings with pliers.

7 Hold the free ends of the chains together and join them using a jump ring. Join the jump ring to an S-joiner and close the ring very tightly. Attach a key ring to the top of the S-joiner to make a hanger.

8 Glue green glass nuggets around the outside of the chandelier. Glue a red glass nugget to the outside of each can.

A Hindu temple was the inspiration for this charming little ornamental shrine assembled from an assortment of tins. Hang it among the branches of a tree in your garden.

Shimmering Temple

you will need

tin cans in assorted sizes

can opener

protective gloves

tin shears or snips

mallet

pencil

hole punch

scrap wood and wooden block

drill

pop riveter and rivets

pliers

scrap of metal lawn-edging (optional)

galvanized wire

wire cutters

self-healing cutting mat

centre punch

hammer

3 fluted petit four tins in different sizes

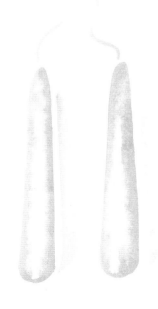

1 Remove the ends from two cans, including the reinforced rims. Wash and dry the cans thoroughly. Wearing protective gloves, cut the cans open with tin shears or snips and flatten with a mallet. Mark windows and a door on one can with a pencil. Pierce with a hole punch, working on a piece of scrap wood. Cut out the shapes with tin shears or snips.

2 Fold each side over a block of wood and hammer with a mallet. The centre panel needs to be wider than the diameter of the can that will stand on top of the box you are making. Repeat with the second can, omitting the doors and the windows. Drill holes through the side panels of both of the sections and pop rivet them together to form the lower box section.

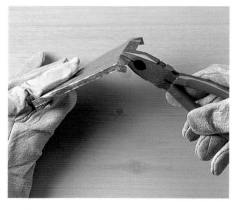

3 Cut a tin rectangle from another flattened can, slightly larger than the box you have made. Turn down all four sides with pliers, clipping the corners to form a lid.

4 Remove the lids, although not the bottoms, from two smaller cans (use two with different proportions). Mark out windows, pierce and cut, making sure the closed end is at the top.

5 Cut a cuff from a piece of flattened can and scallop the edge. Bend into a circle slightly larger than one of the small tins and pop rivet together.

6 Cut a circle from a flattened can or large lid. Scallop the edge all round using tin shears or snips. Fold down each scallop with pliers.

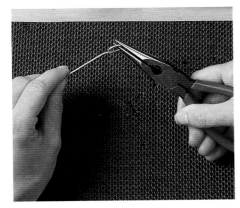

7 Make a base from a scrap of lawn-edging or a large flattened can. Fold up the side edges with pliers. Cut a long piece of galvanized wire and bend the end into a loop.

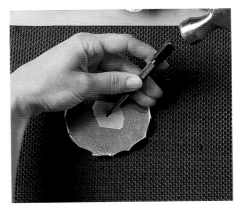

8 Cut a rectangle of ridged tin to sit on top of the lid of the bottom section. Scallop the edge. Bend the front edge up at 90°. Centre punch a hole through all the components, including the petit four tins.

9 To assemble the house, start with the base and thread the wire through all the sections. At the top, trim away any excess wire and bend the top into a hook for hanging.

Practical

Tinwork

Metal is hardwearing, strong and durable, and ideal for using to create a variety of essential items around the home. You can make an enormous range of exciting projects, from cutlery boxes, lunchboxes and mailboxes, to coat racks and spice racks, clocks and cabinets, and even a hammered weathervane to attach to your roof. This extremely versatile and attractive material can be used to meet many of your domestic requirements.

Steely Surfaces

Metal is an ideal material to use around the home. It is strong, sturdy, easy to clean and also looks good. Choose from the bright shine of aluminium, the soft glow of copper, or the hammered look of pewter. Alternatively, you can paint or burnish metal to achieve a different effect altogether. Working with metal is not too difficult, but you may need to practise on spare pieces of metal before you launch straight into a

project. Creating a pewter-effect shelf, for example, may sound easy, but to achieve a professional-looking finish requires considerable dexterity. Likewise, creating a punched metal cabinet front may simply appear to be a case of tracing around a stencil, then punching a line of dots around the traced line. However, ensuring that all the punched dots look regular and even does

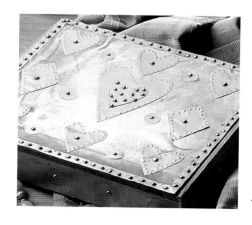

require a certain amount of skill with a centre punch. Nevertheless, if you take your time and are prepared to practise, you will achieve wonderful results and enjoy the great sense of satisfaction that comes with acquiring a new skill.

In this chapter you can learn how to make a wide variety of functional metal boxes for your home, ranging from jewellery boxes and cutlery boxes to mailboxes, in addition to clocks, doorstops, number plaques, birdbaths, suitcases, buckets and a stylish herb planter. The projects range from simple to more complex, so make sure that you choose a project suitable for your skill level.

The metals used in this chapter range from thin zinc sheet to recycled oil drums and anything in between. When cutting metal, you need to wear goggles and thick protective gloves as the cut edges of metal can be very sharp. All the projects involve

the use of special tools, such as tin snips, hide hammers and pop riveters. If you have never used any of these tools before, don't be put off by them; once you have experimented with them, you will find they are easy to manipulate. Using the right tool for the right job will ensure your projects are made accurately and with as good a finish as you would want.

You will have endless pleasure watching birds preening and cleaning themselves in this beautiful beaten copper birdbath. Keep a fresh water supply to ensure the health and happiness of the birds.

Copper Birdbath

you will need

chinagraph pencil

string

copper sheet, 0.9mm/¹⁄₂₇in thick

protective gloves

tin shears

file

blanket

hammer

medium copper wire, 4m/13ft long

bench vice

cup hook

drill and 3mm/¹⁄₈in bit

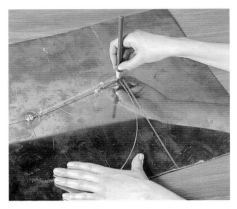

1 Using a chinagraph pencil and looped string, mark a 45cm/17¾in circle on the copper. Wearing gloves, cut out the circle with tin shears. File the sharp edges smooth.

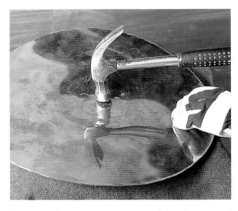

2 Put the copper on a blanket and hammer it lightly from the centre. Spread the dips out to the rim. Repeat, starting from the centre each time, to get the required shape.

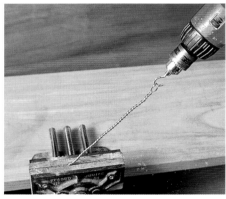

3 To make the perch, double a 1m/40in length of wire and hold the ends in a vice. Fasten a cup hook into the chuck of a hand drill and loop it through the wire. Twist the wire with the drill, then drill three 3mm/¹⁄₈in holes around the rim of the birdbath. Bend a knot into one end of three 1m/40in lengths of wire. Thread the wires up through the holes. Slip the perch over two of the straight wires.

This project fuses the clarity of high-tech design with the quirkiness of surrealist sculpture – and it provides an ideal place to keep your cutlery at the same time!

Cutlery Box

you will need

small silver-plated knife, fork and
spoon, polished
3 metal boxes with lids
permanent marker pen
coarse-grade sandpaper (glasspaper)
file
metal-bonding compound
craft knife

1 Bend the knife to a right angle halfway along the handle. It should bend easily, but if not, do it over the edge of a table. Place the knife on one of the boxes and mark its position. Roughen the contact point on the knife with sandpaper. Rub the part of the lid that will make contact with the knife handle with a file.

2 Mix the metal-bonding compound, following the instructions supplied. Apply the bonding to the area on the lid that has been roughened. The knife is fixed only at this point, so the bond needs to be strong.

3 Press the knife handle firmly into position on the bonding. Use a fine instrument, such as a craft knife, to remove any surrounding bonding compound. Repeat to add the fork and spoon to the other boxes.

If you want to jazz up an old piece of furniture, corrugated metal lawn edging is perfect for the job. Simply find the most suitable width of edging, cut it to size and screw it to the drawer fronts.

Metal-faced Drawers

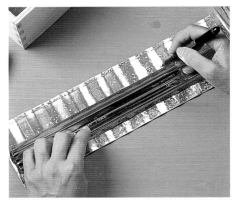

1 Measure the fronts of the drawers. Transfer these dimensions to the lawn edging with a marker pen. Wearing protective gloves, cut the metal lawn edging to size using tin snips or shears.

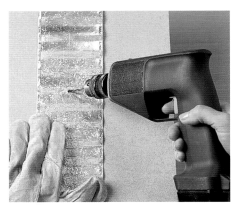

2 Clamp each metal strip to a piece of scrap board and drill a hole in all four corners of the metal strips and in the centre for the drawer handles or knobs.

3 Place the metal on the front of the drawer and then mark the positions of the holes with a marker pen.

4 Drill holes in the four corners of the drawer front. Screw the metal strip to the drawer at each drilled hole.

5 Finally, screw a decorative handle to the centre front of each drawer.

Minimalist detail and smooth contours give this clock a sophisticated look of industrial chic. It would look ideal in a chrome kitchen where the shiny aluminium would add a reflective quality.

Contemporary Clock

you will need

2 aluminium ring moulds

drill

clock mechanism with extra long shank

screwdriver

paper

pencil

scissors

strong glue

4 square nuts, 1cm/²⁄₅in wide

double-sided adhesive pads

1 Choose two ring moulds that fit well together. Drill a hole in the centre of the smaller mould to take the shank for the clock hands.

2 Insert the clock mechanism and screw in place. Make sure the hands will fit inside the rim of the small ring mould.

3 Draw around the smallest end of the large mould and cut out the paper circle. Fold it carefully into quarters, unfold it and lay on top of the mould. Make a light pencil mark on the mould at each quarter line.

4 Using strong glue, carefully fix a square nut at each quarter mark on the larger mould.

5 Fix the small mould into the larger one using adhesive pads. Mount the clock on the wall.

This jewel box is made from a combination of thin zinc sheet, which has a subtle sheen rather like pewter, and brass shim, which is a fairly soft metal used mostly by sculptors.

Jewel Box

you will need

work shirt and protective
leather gloves

tin shears and snips

thin zinc plate

old cigar box

file

pencil

thin cardboard

scissors

brass shim

sheet of chipboard

hammer and nail

soldering mat

protective mask and goggles

soldering iron and solder

strong glue

1 Wearing a work shirt and protective gloves, use tin shears to cut a piece of zinc to cover the lid of the cigar box. The zinc should be slightly larger than the box lid, to allow for a rim to cover the edges of the lid. File any rough edges. Draw a diamond and two different-sized hearts on a sheet of thin cardboard and cut them out.

2 Place the templates on a piece of brass shim and draw around them – six small hearts, one large heart and two diamonds. Draw some small circles freehand. Draw one small heart on a scrap of zinc. Cut out all the shapes and file the edges smooth. Place them on the chipboard and stamp a line of dots around the edge of each using a hammer and nail. Do not stamp the circles and zinc heart.

◄ **3** Cut four strips of shim to make a border around the zinc lid cover. Place all the pieces on a soldering mat and, wearing a protective mask and goggles, drop a blob of liquid solder in the centre of the circles, small hearts and diamonds. Cover the zinc heart with solder blobs. Add a line of blobs to each piece of the shim border.

4 Turn down a narrow rim around the zinc panel at 90° to turn down over the sides of the lid. Glue all the shapes and the borders to the panel.

5 Cut a strip of zinc the width of the box side and long enough to fit all around. File the edges smooth. Cut circles of shim, decorate each with a blob of solder and glue in place.

6 Glue the zinc strip around the sides of the box. Glue the zinc panel to the top of the lid. Gently tap the edges of the panel to make them flush with the sides of the lid.

Aluminium flashing, generally used in roofing, takes on an unusual, pitted appearance that resembles pewter when it is hammered. It can be used to cover simple shapes such as this shelf.

Pewter-look Shelf

you will need

paper

pencil

ruler

scissors

sheet of MDF (medium-density fibreboard), 18mm/³⁄₄ in thick

hand saw

drill

wood glue

2 screws

screwdriver

aluminium flashing

craft knife

ball hammer

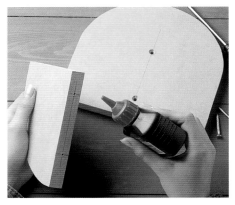

1 Mark the two shelf pieces on MDF, using the template. Cut them out with a hand saw. Draw a line down the centre and mark two points for the drill holes. Mark corresponding points on the long edge of the stand. Drill holes at these points, then glue and screw the shelf and stand together.

2 Cut lengths of aluminium flashing roughly to size using a craft knife. Peel away the backing and stick them to the shelf top, trimming the rough edges at the side with a craft knife and ruler as you go. Join each new length of flashing very closely to the last, so that no MDF is visible beneath the covering.

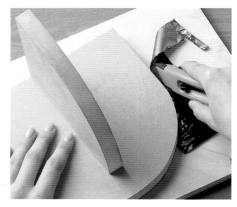

3 When the top is covered, place the shelf face down on a large piece of scrap MDF and trim away the excess flashing using a craft knife.

4 Cut lengths of flashing to cover the back and sides of the shelf, and stick them in place.

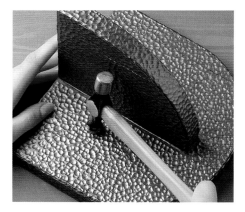

5 Using a ball hammer, tap the surface of the flashing to make indentations close together. Vary the force with which you strike the flashing, to make an interesting and irregular pattern.

This punched tin cabinet is based on those of the American settlers, who produced a wide range of household artefacts using tin plate and, in doing so, raised the decorative punching process to an art form.

Punched Panel Cabinet

you will need

small wooden cabinet with a recess in the door

ruler

sheet of tin plate, 30 gauge (0.3mm/¹⁄₈₃in thick)

permanent marker pen

work shirt and protective leather gloves

tin shears

90° and 45° wooden blocks

bench vice

hide hammer

file

pair of compasses (compass)

pencil

graph paper

scissors

sheet of chipboard

panel pins (tacks)

tack hammer

masking tape

centre punch

ball hammer

small chisel

1 Measure the recess in the door of the cabinet. Mark out the dimensions of the recess on the tin using a marker pen. Draw a 1cm/²⁄₅in border inside the rectangle. Mark points along the sides 2cm/⁴⁄₅in from each corner of the outer rectangle. Draw diagonal lines from these points to the corners of the inner rectangle.

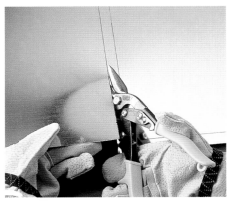

2 Wearing a work shirt and protective leather gloves, cut the panel from the sheet of tin using tin shears. Cut along the diagonal lines at the corners. This will allow the border to be folded behind the panel to give it a smooth edge.

3 Firmly clamp the 90° block of wood in the bench vice. Place the panel on the wooden block with the ruled edge of the tin resting on the edge of the block. Using a hide hammer, tap along the edge of the panel to turn it over to an angle of 90°.

4 Turn the panel over. Position the 45° wooden block inside the turned edge and hammer the edge over it. Remove the block and hammer the edge flat. Finish the remaining sides of the panel in the same way. File the corners to remove any sharp edges.

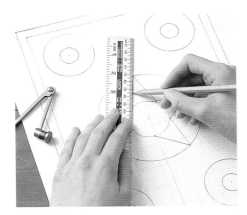

5 Using a pair of compasses (compass) and a ruler, measure out and draw the panel design on graph paper. Cut the paper to the same size as the panel.

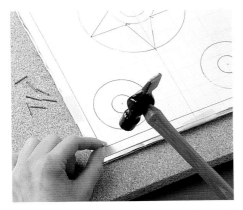

6 Place the panel face up on a sheet of chipboard and secure each corner to the board with a panel pin (tack). Tape the paper pattern to the front of the panel.

7 Place the centre punch on one of the lines. Tap it with the hammer to indent the tin. Move the punch along the line and tap it to make the next mark. Complete the design.

8 Remove the paper pattern and add extra decoration to the front of the panel using a small chisel. Unpin the panel from the board.

9 Place the decorated panel in the recess on the front of the cabinet. Use panel pins at each corner to attach the panel securely to the cabinet.

Pewter shim is simple to emboss. For this project, a wooden block is wrapped like a parcel with the embossed pewter to make an attractive doorstop – you could also use it as an unusual bookend.

Scrollwork Doorstop

you will need

pewter shim, 38 x 39cm/15 x 15½in

self-healing cutting mat

permanent marker pen

ruler

dry ballpoint pen

embossing stylus

ice lolly (popsicle) stick

pencil

wooden block, 19 x 9 x 9cm/
7½ x 3½ x 3½in

2 metal washers, 4cm/1½in diameter

hammer

2 roofing nails

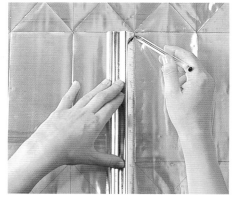

1 Place the pewter shim on a cutting mat. Following the template at the back of the book, use a marker pen and ruler to draw the foldlines on to the metal. Using a dry ballpoint pen, score a line 3mm/⅛in from one end and fold over. Score along all the solid marked lines. Turn the pewter over and score the remaining dotted lines.

2 Turn the sheet back again and use a permanent marker pen to draw the pattern in freehand on the areas shown on the template. Vary the design according to your personal taste. If you are using a more formal design than these freestyle curlicues, plan it on paper first. This is the back of the design.

3 Score the pattern on the pewter with a stylus. Use an ice lolly stick end for thick lines and a pencil for fine ones.

4 Turn the sheet over and complete the design by indenting dots around the lines using the stylus or pencil.

5 Wrap the shim around the wooden block, allowing the neatened, folded edge to overlap the other edge. Make sure you place the block centrally, with equal amounts for folding.

6 Fold along the scored lines and wrap up the block as if it were a present.

7 Place a metal washer centrally on the end of the block and hammer a roofing nail through it to secure the pewter and give it interesting detail. Repeat at the other end of the block.

The rising sun has been incorporated into the design of this number plaque. Small indentations are punched into the front of the plaque to create a densely pitted surface and to raise the unpunched areas.

Number Plaque

you will need

sheet of tin plate, 30 gauge
(0.3mm/¹⁄₈₃in thick)

permanent marker pen

ruler

work shirt and protective
leather gloves

tin shears

90° and 45° wooden blocks

bench vice

hide hammer

file

graph paper

scissors

pencil

masking tape

sheet of chipboard

panel pins (tacks)

tack hammer

centre punch

ball hammer

wire (steel) wool

clear polyurethane varnish

varnish brush

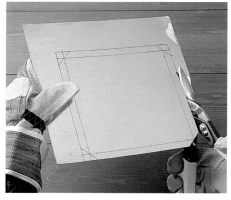

1 Draw a rectangle on a sheet of tin. Draw a 1cm/²⁄₅in border around the inside of the rectangle. Measure a point 2.5cm/1in from each corner of the outer rectangle. Draw diagonal lines across all the corners. Wearing protective clothing, cut out the plaque with tin shears.

2 Firmly clamp the 90° block of wood in a bench vice. Place the plaque on the wooden block with the ruled edge of the tin resting on the edge of the block. Using a hide hammer, tap along the edge of the plaque to turn over all the marked border areas to an angle of 90°.

3 Turn the plaque over and position the 45° wooden block inside the turned edge. Hammer the edge over it, remove the block and then hammer the edge completely flat. Finish the remaining three sides of the plaque in the same way. Carefully file the four corners to make them smooth.

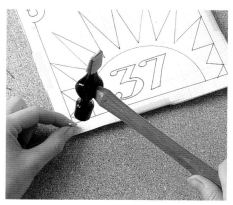

4 Cut a piece of graph paper the same size as the plaque. Draw your pattern and desired numbers, then tape the pattern to the front of the plaque. Secure it to the chipboard with a panel pin (tack) in each corner.

5 Place the centre punch on a line and tap it with a ball hammer to make an indentation. Move the punch about 3mm/⅛in along the line and tap it again to make the next mark. Continue to punch along the lines until the design is completed.

6 Remove the paper pattern, then randomly punch the surface around the sunburst and inside the numbers. Scour the surface of the panel with wire (steel) wool before sealing the plaque with varnish. Allow to dry before screwing in place.

The gently sloping sides of a dustbin (garbage can) lid allow smaller birds to paddle in the shallow water, while larger birds can splash in the middle without emptying the water.

Chrome Birdbath

you will need

hacksaw

galvanized dustbin (garbage can) lid

pliers

protective gloves

cylindrical metal cheese grater

round fence post to suit size of grater

galvanized nails

hammer

night-light

1 Using a hacksaw, saw across the middle of the dustbin (garbage can) lid's handle. Bend back both sides of the severed handle using pliers.

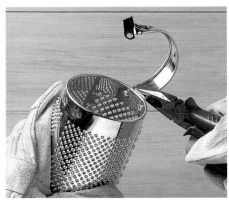

2 Wearing protective gloves, remove the handle from the top of the metal cheese grater using the pliers.

3 Push the narrow end of the cheese grater on to the fence post and secure it with galvanized nails through the holes left by the handle rivets.

4 Squeeze the sides of the lid handle together to insert them in the wide end of the grater. Place a night-light inside the grater to stop the water in the birdbath from freezing.

Punched tin designs are a staple technique of folk-art interiors, but they are often kept to quite small areas. However, used over a larger area, punched tin will look much more dramatic.

Punched Tin Folk-art Wall

1 Design and draw the pattern for the punched tin wall to scale on paper. Cut a piece of tin sheet to size using tin shears and wearing protective gloves. Using a metal file, smooth any rough edges.

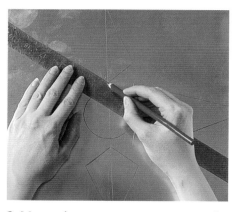

2 Using the paper pattern as a guide, draw the design to the correct size on the reverse side of the metal sheet using a chinagraph pencil and long metal ruler. Make sure any repeated straight lines are parallel.

3 Using a metal punch and a tack hammer, practise punching on a spare scrap of metal to get a feel for how hard you need to punch.

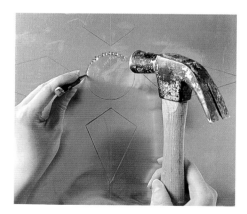

4 Place an offcut of wood behind the tin to protect your work surface. Then punch out the pattern. Drill holes in the corners of the metal sheet.

5 Using a carpenter's spirit level and straight edge, draw lines on the wall to show the position of the sheet. Drill holes for the corners. Insert wall plugs (plastic anchors).

6 Screw the metal sheet in position on the wall. Coat the metal sheet with a protective layer of varnish or lacquer to protect it against rust.

This ingenious workshop accessory efficiently dispenses different kinds of string from its three funnels. Its brilliant patchwork background is made from a collection of colourful printed tin cans.

String Dispenser

you will need

assorted printed tin cans

can opener

protective gloves

tin shears

mallet

length of wood, 10 x 2cm/4 x ⅘in

self-healing cutting mat

nails

hammer

ruler

3 metal funnels

permanent marker pen

drill

2 mirror fixing plates

screws

screwdriver

3 balls of string

◀ **1** Remove the lids and bottoms from the cans including the reinforced rims. Wash them and leave to dry. Wearing protective gloves, cut the cans open with tin shears and flatten them using a mallet. Select two cans slightly wider than the length of wood. Working on a cutting mat, nail them to each end of the wood so that they overlap the edges, as shown.

2 Clip the corners of the cans diagonally with tin shears. Fold them neatly over the edges of the wood. Hammer the edges down flat with the mallet, then nail in place.

3 Arrange the other cans along the wood until you are satisfied with the arrangement. Nail in place to cover the wood, overlapping them slightly. Fold over the edges as before and nail to secure.

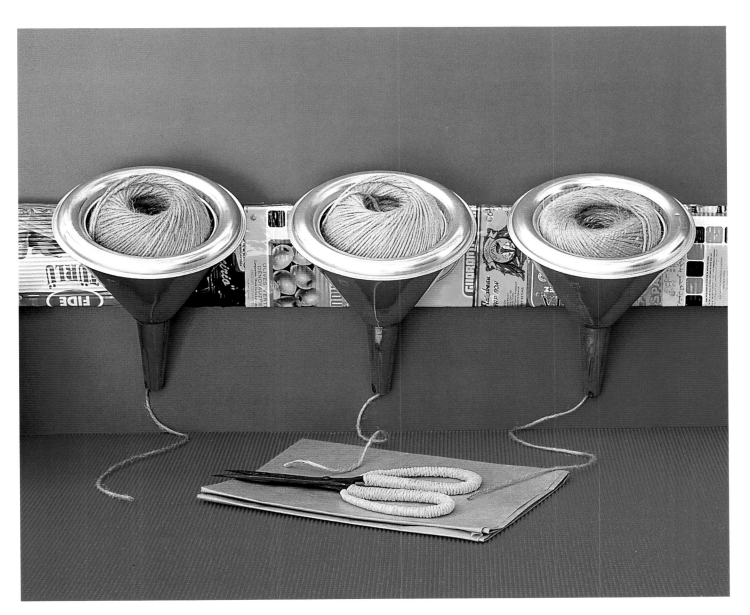

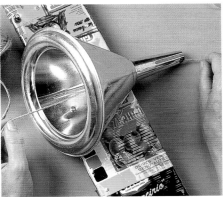

4 Measure the finished panel to work out the position of each funnel. Mark with a marker pen. Drill a guide hole at each marked point. Turn the panel over and attach two mirror fixing plates at the back for hanging.

5 Drill a hole in identical positions in each of the funnels, so that the top edges align. Screw the funnels into the guide holes on the panel.

6 Put a ball of string into each funnel and thread the end (taken from the centre of the ball) through the spout. Attach the string dispenser to the wall as required.

Turn an ordinary tin into a stylish suitcase with webbing straps and a smart handle. Embellish the case by attaching a foil plaque embossed with your name or initials.

Stylish Suitcase

you will need

metal drawer or cupboard handle

rectangular metal tin with hinged lid

ruler

permanent marker pen

clamp

drill

nuts and bolts (or rivets)

screwdriver (or pop riveter)

narrow luggage webbing straps

scissors

hole punch or bradawl (awl)

1 Centre the handle on the side of the tin opposite the hinges and mark the fixing positions using a permanent marker pen.

2 Securely clamp the case to the work surface in preparation for drilling the holes for the handle. Use wooden supports as shown.

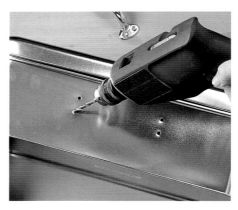

3 Drill handle holes. Mark and drill two strap holes midway between the box sides and the handle fixings. Drill two holes in corresponding positions on the hinge side of the tin case.

4 Attach the handle with small nuts and bolts (or you could use rivets).

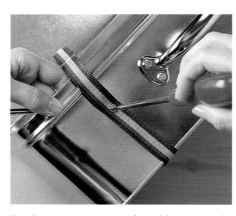

5 Cut two strips of webbing to fit around the box and mark them with the positions of the drilled holes. Punch a small hole at each marked point and attach the straps in the same way as the handle.

Unwanted food containers are a good source of metal and are perfect for making items such as this handsome spice rack, as they are already partly formed into the right shape.

Spice Rack

you will need

work shirt and protective leather gloves

biscuit (cookie) tin

tin shears

file

permanent marker pen

masking tape

soldering mat

protective mask and goggles

flux

soldering iron and solder

pliers

ruler or tape measure

fine wire

wire cutters

wooden block

bradawl (awl)

scrap of brass shim

strong glue

1 Wearing protective clothes, cut the base of the biscuit (cookie) tin in half carefully using tin shears. File all the cut edges of the tin smooth. You will only need one half of the tin for this project. Dispose of the other half safely.

2 Draw the curved shape of the back panel of the spice rack on to the lid of the tin. Cut out using tin shears and file all the cut edges smooth. Place the curved back panel against the cut edge of one half of the biscuit tin. Hold the two together with masking tape.

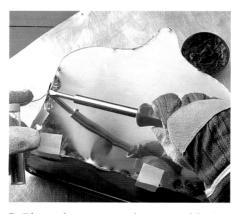

3 Place the spice rack on a soldering mat. Wearing a protective mask and goggles, apply flux to the join, then solder the two parts together. Using pliers, fold in the filed edges of the back panel and the base to flatten them completely. File any remaining rough edges smooth.

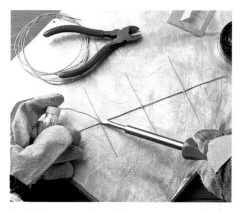

4 Measure the dimensions of the inside of the spice rack. Cut lengths of fine wire and solder them together to make a grid to form compartments for the spices. Place the grid inside the spice rack and solder it in place.

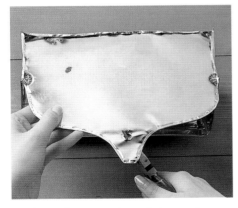

5 Place the top edge of the rack on a block of wood and pierce a hole in it using a bradawl (awl). Open the hole slightly using a pair of pliers. File the rough edges from the inside hole. Turn over the edges around the hole and squeeze them flat with pliers.

6 Cut a length of fine wire and form a spiral at each end. Cut six lengths of wire and form two large and two small curves and two small circles. Solder the spiral to the back of the rack and the curves to the front. Shape a wire to fit around the edges of the back of the rack and solder in place.

7 Cut a small circle of brass shim and glue it to the centre back of the rack. Apply decorative blobs of solder to the shim circle, along the edge of the rack, around the spiral and in the small circles. Make a wire circle to go around the shim and solder in place.

You don't need metal-working skills to make this cheerful weathervane, as the shapes are cut out of rigid plastic sheet and covered with strips of roof-flashing, which is given a densely pitted texture.

Hammered Weathervane

you will need

paper

pencil

ruler

scissors

permanent marker pen

rigid plastic sheet (Plexiglas)

coping saw, jigsaw or band saw

scrap wood

drill

craft knife

small paint roller

galvanized wire

aluminium flashing

metal straight edge

hacksaw

file

brass screw

screwdriver

metal rod or broom handle

newspaper

small ball hammer

blue glass paint

paintbrush

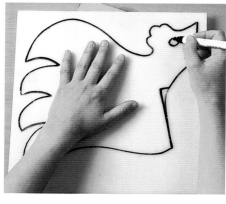

1 Scale up the template at the back of the book and cut out paper patterns for the rooster and an arrow 24cm/ 9½ in long. Draw around these shapes on to the plastic sheet.

2 Cut out the shapes using a coping saw, jigsaw or band saw. Using a piece of scrap wood to protect your work surface, drill a row of small holes as shown. Drill the rooster's eye.

3 Use a craft knife to cut the central plastic tube from a small paint roller and use galvanized wire to attach it to the rooster.

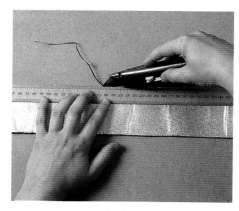

4 Cut strips of aluminium flashing long enough to cover the plastic shapes. Trim the edges of the strips using a craft knife and straight edge, so that you can make neat joints.

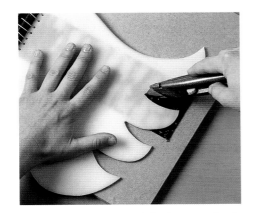

5 Apply the strips of flashing to both sides of the rooster, trimming the edges with a craft knife as you stick them on. Wrap the lower strips on the rooster around the roller.

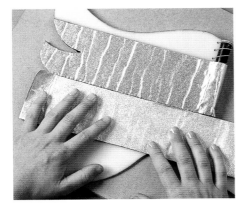

6 As you apply further strips, join the long edges together carefully. Cut out the eye of the rooster. Cover the arrow with flashing, then drill a small hole for the screw.

7 Using a hacksaw, remove the bent section of the paint roller handle. File the sawn edges smooth.

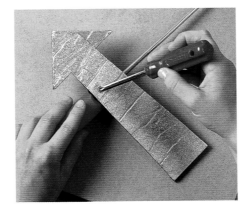

8 Screw the arrow to the plastic roller handle. Fit the roller handle to the metal rod or broom handle to make a mount for the weathervane.

9 Working on newspaper, tap gently all over the bird to give it texture. Colour the section marked on the template blue. Attach the rooster.

A coat rack will keep coats, umbrellas and hats tidy, avoiding clutter in halls. The rich purple background and the slightly matt tones of the metal foils give this rack a touch of splendour.

Regal Coat Rack

you will need
pencil
graph paper
ruler or tape measure
scissors
sheet of MDF (medium-density fibreboard), 5mm/¼ in thick
hand saw or jigsaw
fine-grade sandpaper (glasspaper)
wood primer
paintbrush
satin-finish wood paint
tracing paper
soft pencil
thin cardboard
copper foil, 40 gauge (0.08mm/¹⁄₃₀₀in thick)
dry ballpoint pen
aluminium foil, 36 gauge (0.1mm/¹⁄₂₅₀in thick)
centre punch
epoxy resin glue
drill
3 ball end hooks
2 mirror plates

1 Draw the basic shape for the coat rack on to graph paper to make a pattern. This rack is 60cm/23½ in wide by 20cm/8in high at its highest point. Cut out and draw around it on to the MDF. Saw out the shape with a hand saw or jigsaw. Smooth the edges with sandpaper (glasspaper).

2 Seal the surface of the coat rack with one coat of wood primer. When it is dry, lightly sand the surface, then paint it with satin-finish wood paint. Allow to dry thoroughly. Trace the crown, fleur-de-lys and star templates from the back of the book. Transfer them on to a sheet of thin cardboard. Cut out the shapes to make templates.

3 Place the crown on the copper foil and draw around it using a dry ball-point pen. Repeat. Draw around the fleur-de-lys and stars on aluminium foil. Draw two stars. Cut out all of the shapes using scissors.

4 Rest each shape on a piece of thin cardboard. Make a line of dots around the edge of all the shapes by pressing into the foil using a centre punch.

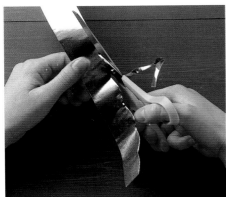

5 Cut a 5cm/2in-wide strip of the aluminium foil the same length as the bottom edge of the rack. Cut a wavy line along the top edge of the strip and then mark a row of dots along it with the punch.

6 Place the wavy edging and the stars, crowns and fleur-de-lys on the front of the rack with the raised side of the dots facing upwards. Use epoxy resin glue to stick the pieces in place.

7 When the glue is thoroughly dry, drill three holes at equal distances 2.5cm/1in from the bottom edge of the coat rack. Screw a hook into each hole. Attach a mirror plate to both sides of the coat rack for hanging.

This delightful clock is made from copper sheet and wire on a base of self-hardening clay and is decorated with paint and gold pigment. This novel timepiece is sure to amuse your friends.

Magic Wand Clock

you will need

tin shears or snips

copper wire

copper sheet

pair of compasses (compass)

thin cardboard

pliers

fretsaw (scroll saw)

aluminium tube, 1cm/²⁄₅in diameter, 40cm/15¾in long

self-hardening clay

rolling pin

sharp modelling tool

terracotta-coloured acrylic paint

paintbrushes

clear acrylic varnish

gold powder pigment

clock movement and hands

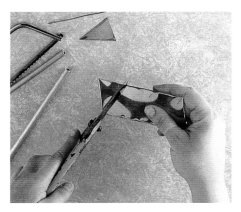

1 Using tin shears or snips, cut five 20cm/8in lengths of copper wire and four 18cm/7in lengths. Cut out five triangles and one heart shape from the copper sheet. Draw a circle 11.5cm/4½in in diameter on cardboard and cut out. Draw a second circle inside with a diameter of 6cm/2½in and cut out the centre.

2 Using pliers, bend the shorter pieces of wire into zigzag shapes with looped ends and four of the longer ones into spirals. Bend the top ends of the wire over slightly. Using a fretsaw (scroll saw), cut the aluminium tube into two pieces, one piece measuring 10cm/4in, the other measuring 30cm/12in.

3 Roll out the clay and place the circle template on top. Using a modelling tool, cut two clay discs, one using the outer edge only, the other including the inner circle as well. While the clay is wet, embed the copper triangles around the edge of the solid circle.

4 Stick the zigzags and spirals into the clay, alternating them between the triangles. Place the short aluminium tube at the bottom of the circle. Place the hollow disc on top so that it fits flush with the solid one. Press them together and remove the tube.

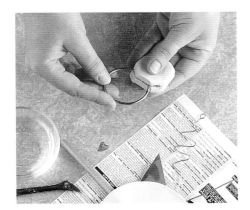

5 Roll out the leftover clay and cut out two hexagons. Bend a length of copper wire into a loop and insert between the two hexagons. Insert one end of the longer aluminium tube between the hexagons and press them together. Fit the other end of the tube into the moulded hole made by the shorter tube in the head of the clock. Press the metal heart into the centre of the top hexagon. Make a hole in the circle for the clock movement and leave all parts of the clock to dry for two to three days.

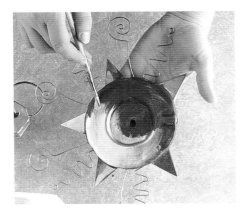

6 When dry, prime the clay with the terracotta-coloured paint. Leave it to dry. Mix clear acrylic varnish with gold powder pigment and paint over the terracotta-coloured areas and the tube. Fit the clock movement and hands and, to finish, wind copper wire up around the aluminium tube.

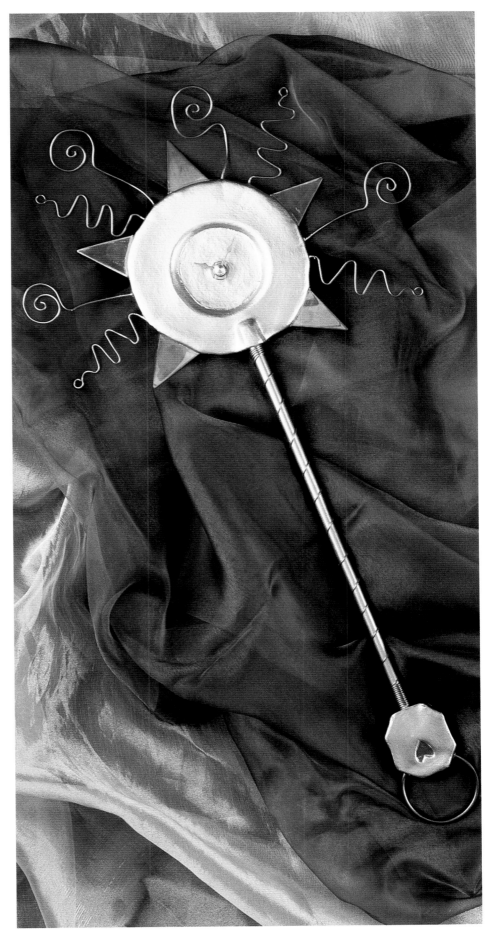

Add a touch of fairy-tale romance to your garden with this whimsical tower. Secure it to a tray on top of a tree stump or post, and sprinkle bird food all around.

Rapunzel's Tower

you will need

paper

pencil

garden twine

ruler or tape measure

scissors

metal tubing, 15cm/6in diameter

45 x 45cm/18 x 18in copper sheet,
0.9mm/¹⁄₂₇in thick

chinagraph pencil

protective gloves

tin shears and snips

file

drill, 3mm/⅛in bit

blind rivet gun and 3mm/⅛in rivets

glue gun and glue stick

2.5 x 5cm/1 x 2in copper foil,
0.2mm/¹⁄₁₂₅in thick

nail or wire, 6.5cm/2½in long

twigs

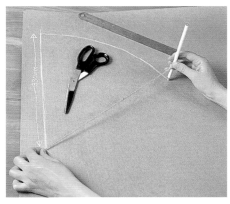

1 Make a pattern for the cone-shaped roof to fit around the metal tubing; add a 2cm/⅘in overlap for joining the edges. Transfer on to the copper sheet with a chinagraph pencil. Wearing protective gloves, cut out the shape using tin shears. File off any sharp edges. Bend the copper into a cone shape with an overlap. Check the fit on the tubing.

2 Drill 3mm/⅛in holes at intervals through both layers of copper along the overlap and fasten the overlap using blind rivets. Squeeze the handle of the rivet gun until the rivet shaft snaps off, securing the overlap firmly. Use a glue gun to glue the cone-shaped roof in place on top of the metal tubing. Allow the glue to dry.

3 Cut a wavy flag for the roof from copper foil. Cut a sideways "V" in one end of the flag and bend the other end around a nail or short piece of wire as a flagpole. Glue to the tip of the roof.

4 Make a rope ladder by knotting cut lengths of small twigs between two pieces of twine. Cut an entrance hole in the tubing with tin snips and glue the ladder in place.

The idea of decorating metal objects with raised punched patterns has been around ever since sheet metal was invented about 300 years ago. Bare metal buckets are ideal for this sort of pattern-making.

Punched Metal Bucket

you will need
permanent marker pen
bare metal bucket
piece of wood
blunt nail or centre punch
hammer
rag
lighter fuel (or similar solvent)

1 Using a permanent marker pen, draw your pattern on the inside of the bucket. Any repeated curves or shapes are suitable.

2 Rest the bucket on a piece of wood to protect the work surface. Following the pattern, tap the nail or centre punch with a hammer, keeping the dents about 1cm/⅖in apart. Hammer the pattern all over the inside.

3 Use a rag and lighter fuel to clean off the marker pen pattern that is left between the punched marks.

Inspired by Mexican folk art, this brilliantly painted and punched mirror frame will give your room a touch of exotic colour and warmth. Use the brightest paints or pens you can find.

Mexican Mirror

you will need

paper

permanent marker pen

scissors

aluminium sheet

glue gun and glue stick

self-healing cutting mat

hammer

small and large centre punches

tin snips

protective gloves

chisel

blue glass paint

paintbrush

permanent felt-tipped pens or
glass paints: turquoise, green,
orange and pink

circular mirror, 15cm/6in diameter

circular cake board, 25cm/10in
diameter

double-sided adhesive pads

nail or fine drill bit

galvanized wire

wire cutters

pliers

7 short screws

screwdriver

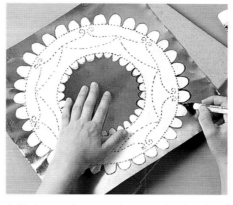

1 Enlarge the template at the back of the book to a diameter of 30cm/12in and then cut it out. Stick the paper pattern to the aluminium sheet using a glue gun, and trace around this with a permanent marker pen.

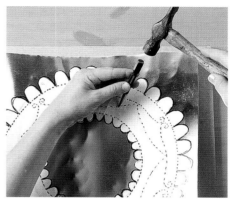

2 With the aluminium sheet resting on a cutting mat, make indentations along the lines of the pattern using a hammer and small centre punch. Just two taps of the hammer at each point should be sufficient.

3 Cut out the shape with tin snips, wearing gloves to protect your hands. To cut out the central area, first punch a hole through the centre using a chisel, and cut from there.

4 Using the small centre punch, hammer indentations at random all over the inner section of the frame to give it an overall texture.

▶

5 Paint the indented section using translucent blue glass paint. Leave to dry. Colour the rest of the frame as shown using permanent felt-tipped pens or glass paints.

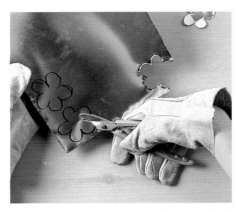

6 Draw and cut out a five-petalled flower template with a diameter of 5cm/2in. Trace all around it on to an aluminium sheet using a permanent marker pen to make seven flowers. Cut them out using tin snips.

7 Colour the individual flowers using permanent felt-tipped pens or glass paints in bright colours.

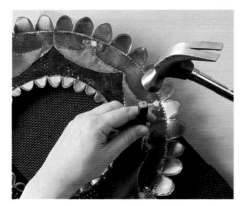

8 Place all the flowers on a cutting mat and use a large centre punch to hammer a hole through the centre of each, big enough for a screw to pass through. If the flowers buckle, bend them back into shape. Make similar holes at all the points on the frame, following the template.

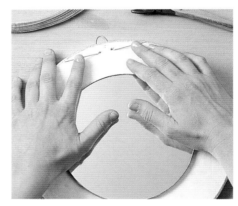

9 Attach the mirror to the bottom of the cake board using double-sided adhesive pads. Pierce two holes near the edge of the board using a nail or fine drill bit. Cut a piece of galvanized wire and bend into a hanging loop. Thread the ends through the holes and bend them flat against the board.

10 Place the frame over the mirror and backing board. Place the flowers in position so that holes correspond with those in the frame and screw them on through the frame into the backing board. Colour the screws to match the flower centres.

Fix this traditionally styled mailbox to your garden gate with its door open. The reflective indicator will tell you at a glance when the door is closed and your post has arrived.

Classic Mailbox

you will need

pencil and ruler

exterior plywood, 18mm/¾in thick

tenon saw

saucer

coping saw, jigsaw or band saw

sandpaper (glasspaper)

tinted exterior varnish (or

polyurethane)

varnish brush

nails

hammer

screws

2 brass screw hinges (spring hinges)

tin shears

protective gloves

cooking-oil drum

metal straight edge

scrap wood

mallet

drill

bicycle reflective indicator

bolt

spanner (wrench)

1 Following the templates at the back of the book, mark the dimensions of the base, back and door on to the plywood surface. Cut out with a tenon saw. Mark the curves by drawing around a saucer.

2 Cut out the curved shapes using a coping saw, jigsaw or band saw. Smooth the edges with sandpaper (glasspaper). Paint all the wooden pieces with tinted exterior varnish (or polyurethane) and leave to dry.

3 Partly hammer nails in the back then hammer the back to the base.

4 Screw the hinges to the door and attach to the front of the wooden base. ▶

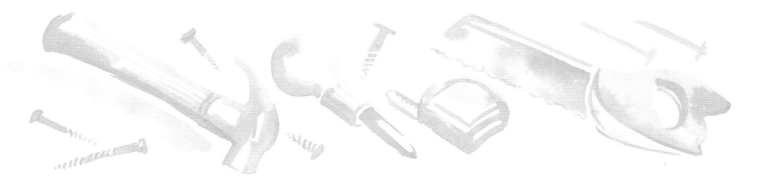

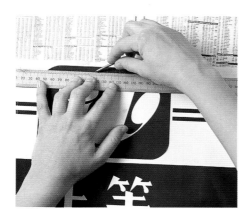

5 Use tin shears to cut off the top and bottom of the oil drum, wearing gloves for protection. Discard carefully. Cut down the seam and flatten the drum. Using the template measurements, mark the metal using a straight edge and a nail, as shown.

6 Cut out the metal sheet using tin shears, wearing gloves to protect your hands. Leave a border all around for turning, as marked on the template.

7 Cut out the small rectangle marked at each of the corners. This enables the edges of the tin to be folded in neatly, without any overlap.

8 Protecting the work surface with some scrap wood, turn in the edges of the metal to eliminate the sharp edges. Tap them flat with a mallet.

9 Pull the metal cover over the base, aligning the edges. Nail the metal to the mailbox base and back, starting at the centre of each side and working outwards. Ensure the door is free.

10 Drill a hole through the door for the indicator and fix it securely in place with a bolt.

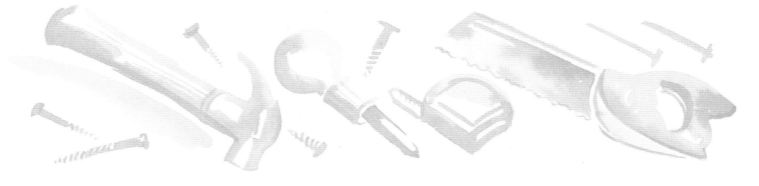

With its distinctive curved lid, this lunch box is based on traditional American designs. The extra space under the box lid makes a handy compartment for storing drinks flasks, which lie on top of the food.

Lunch Box

you will need

work shirt and protective leather gloves

oil drum

hacksaw

tin shears

cloth

ruler

permanent marker pen

90° and 45° wooden blocks

bench vice

hide hammer

file

pliers

fine wire

wire cutters

hammer

drill

G-clamp

MDF (medium-density fibreboard), 18mm/¾in thick

hand saw

red woodstain

paintbrush

2 case locks

screws

screwdriver

bradawl (awl)

nails

nuts and bolts

1 Wearing protective clothes, cut one end from an oil drum using a hacksaw. Using tin shears, cut open the drum and remove the other end to leave a metal panel. Wipe any excess oil from the panel.

2 Using a ruler and marker pen, draw the cover following the template. Using tin shears, cut out the cover.

3 Clamp the 90° block of wood in the vice. Place the cover on it and turn over one edge using a hide hammer. Turn the cover over. Position the 45° wooden block inside the turned edge and hammer the edge over it. Remove the block and hammer the edge flat. Repeat on the other two edges. File all corners smooth. Repeat with the lid.

4 Using pliers, turn alternate tabs of the hinges over. Turn the tabs on each of the two covers so that each folded tab is opposite an unfolded tab. Flatten the tabs using a hide hammer.

▶

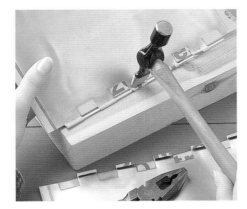

5 Bend half of each unflattened tab back using pliers. Cut a piece of fine wire the same length as the hinge and insert it through the tabs of one of the covers. Hammer the edges of the tabs on this cover firmly under the wire to secure them.

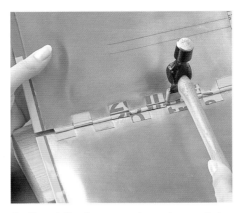

6 Carefully line up the edges of the hinge and slot the remaining tabs under the wire. Fold the tabs around the wire and hammer the ends under as before to finish off the hinge.

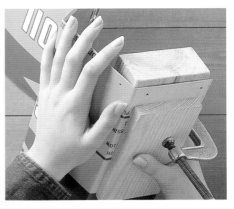

7 Place the cover on a wooden block. Hold the edge with pliers and drill a small hole 9mm/⅜in in from the side edges, and about 2.5cm/1in from the ends, folds and hinge. Drill another hole halfway along the edge of the lid. Place the 90° block inside along a foldline and clamp in place. Bend the cover over. Bend all the folds.

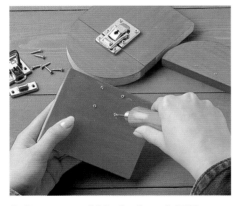

8 Cut two end blocks from MDF using the template as a guide. Cut across each block, as indicated by the dotted line, to create two semi-circles. Stain the wood red. Fit the case locks.

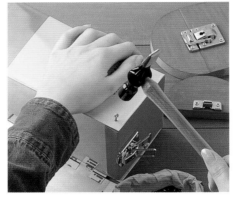

9 Separate the blocks and semi-circles and place the blocks inside the cover. Using a bradawl (awl), mark the nail positions on the blocks through the holes. Nail the cover to the blocks. Place the semi-circles of MDF on top of the blocks and close the catches to hold them. Press the lid around the semi-circles and then nail it securely to the semi-circles.

10 Remove the handle from the oil drum. Place it on a wooden block and drill a hole in each end of the handle. File the holes smooth. Place on top of the lunch box. Using a permanent marker pen, transfer the position of the holes in the handle to the top of the lunch box and drill through. File the holes smooth, then bolt the handle in place.

This brightly painted herb container has an appealing folk-art charm. It is made from recycled tin cans that are hammered flat and soldered together to make a box. The top edges are bound with fine wire.

Herb Container

you will need

can opener

4 tin cans

work shirt and protective
leather gloves

tin shears

sheet of chipboard

hide hammer

file

masking tape

protective mask and goggles

soldering mat

flux

soldering iron and solder

thin tin plate

block of wood

small hammer

bradawl (awl)

fine wire

wire cutters

pliers

wooden pegs (pins)

enamel paints: blue, white, red, yellow
and black

paintbrush

1 Using a can opener, remove the tops and bottoms from four tin cans. Wearing a work shirt and protective gloves, cut the cans open down one side using tin shears. Place the tin panels on a sheet of chipboard and flatten them using a hide hammer. File all the edges of the tin to make them completely smooth.

2 Use one flattened piece of tin to make the base. Bend the other three cans around the base to make a box shape. Hold all the sections together with strips of masking tape. Wearing a protective mask and goggles, put the box on a soldering mat, apply flux to the join and solder the sections of the box together.

3 Cut two long and two short strips of thin tin plate the same lengths as the sides of the box base and file smooth. Arrange each strip along the edge of a long block of wood and hammer it over the wood to make a right angle along its length.

4 Solder the strips of tin around the base of the box and then carefully file all the corners to remove any sharp edges. Using a bradawl (awl), punch two holes in the bottom of the box for drainage and file around the holes to remove the rough edges.

▶

5 Cut three lengths of fine wire long enough to fit around the sides and front of the top of the box. Bend the pieces of wire to the shape of the box and solder together along their lengths. Solder the wire around the side and front edges of the top of the box.

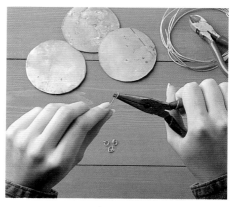

6 To make the flower heads, cut three circles of thin tin about the same size as the tops of the cans. File all the edges smooth. Cut short lengths of wire and twist around the end of a pair of pliers to make seed shapes. Place several seeds on each flower head. Drop a solder dot in the centre of each seed to join it to the head.

7 Solder the flower heads to the back of the box. Hold them in position using wooden pegs (pins) as you work. Cut three lengths of wire long enough to fit around the flower heads. Using your fingers, make long loops of wire for petals. Solder the petals at equal distances along each length of wire.

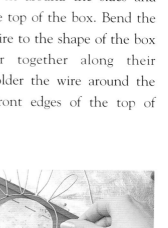
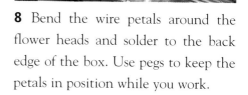

8 Bend the wire petals around the flower heads and solder to the back edge of the box. Use pegs to keep the petals in position while you work.

9 To make the flower stems, cut five lengths of wire the same height as the front and sides of the container. Use your fingers to make six wire leaf shapes for each stem. Solder the leaves to the stems. Solder the stems to the front and sides of the box.

10 Tint the box using blue enamel paint. When it has dried, paint the stems white and the petals red. Paint the flower heads yellow and the seeds black. Paint the strip around the base of the box red.

Templates

Enlarge the templates on a photocopier. Alternatively, trace the design and draw a grid of evenly spaced squares over your tracing. Draw a larger grid on to another piece of paper and copy the outline square by square. Finally, draw over the lines to make sure they are continuous.

Embossed Greetings Cards, p21

Lacy Silver Gloves, p22

Repoussé Frame, p23

Treetop Angel, pp28–29

Candle Collars, pp26–27

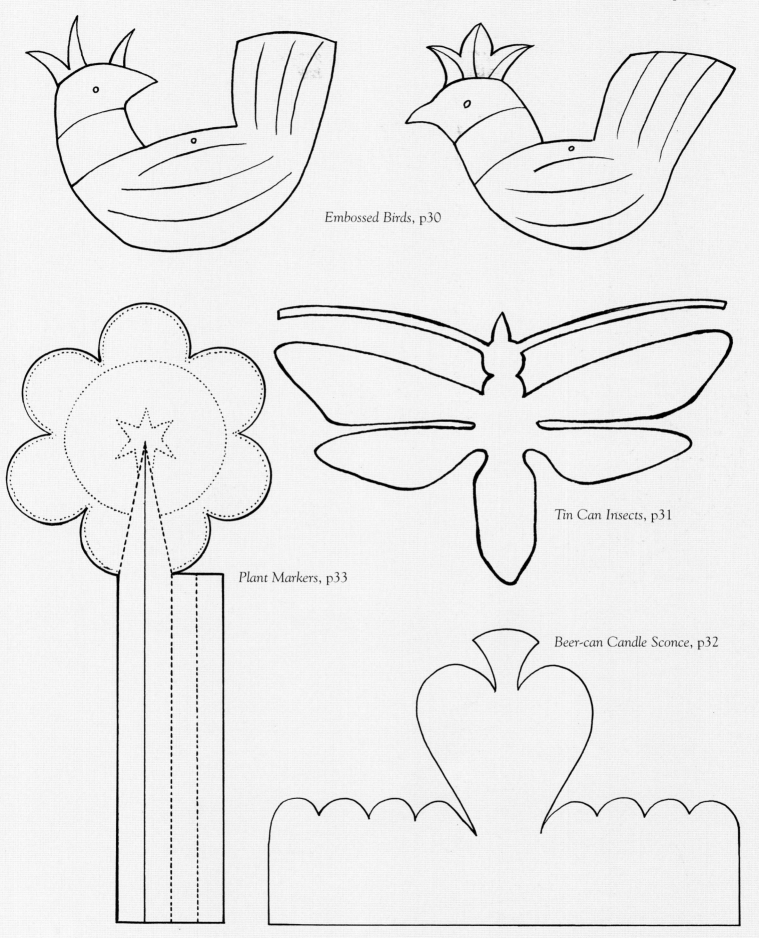

Embossed Birds, p30

Tin Can Insects, p31

Plant Markers, p33

Beer-can Candle Sconce, p32

Bird Chimes, pp58–60

Rocket Candlestick, pp50–51

Metal Reindeer, pp64–65

Pewter-look Shelf, pp82–83

Moorish Flower Blind, pp38–39

Musical Scarecrow, pp61–63

Hammered Weathervane, pp100–101

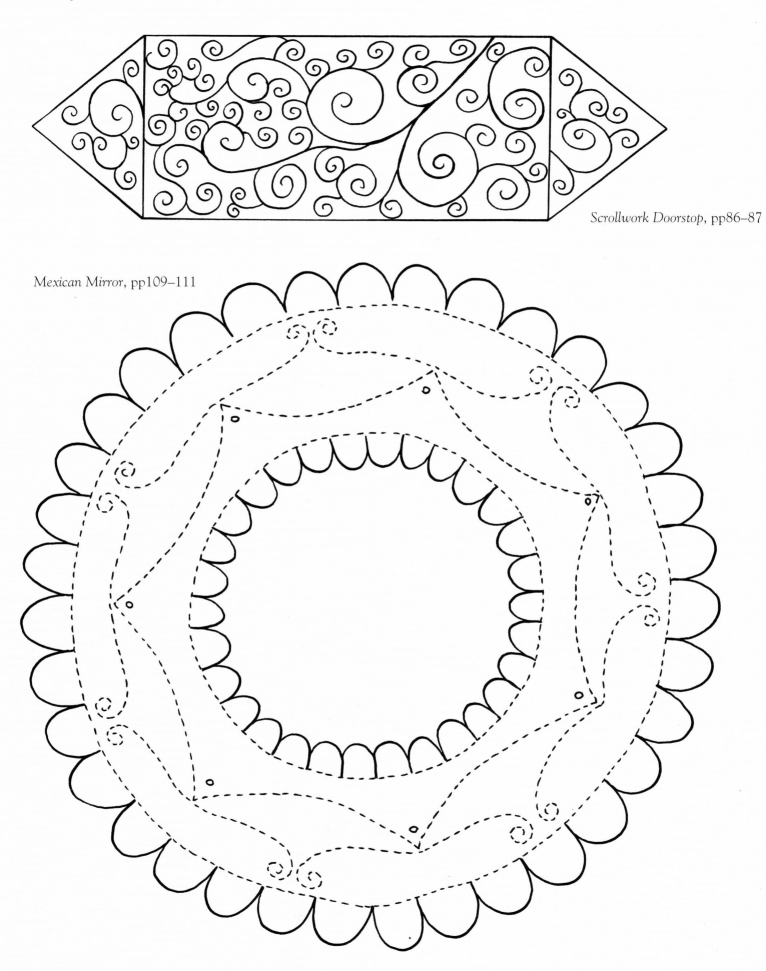

Scrollwork Doorstop, pp86–87

Mexican Mirror, pp109–111

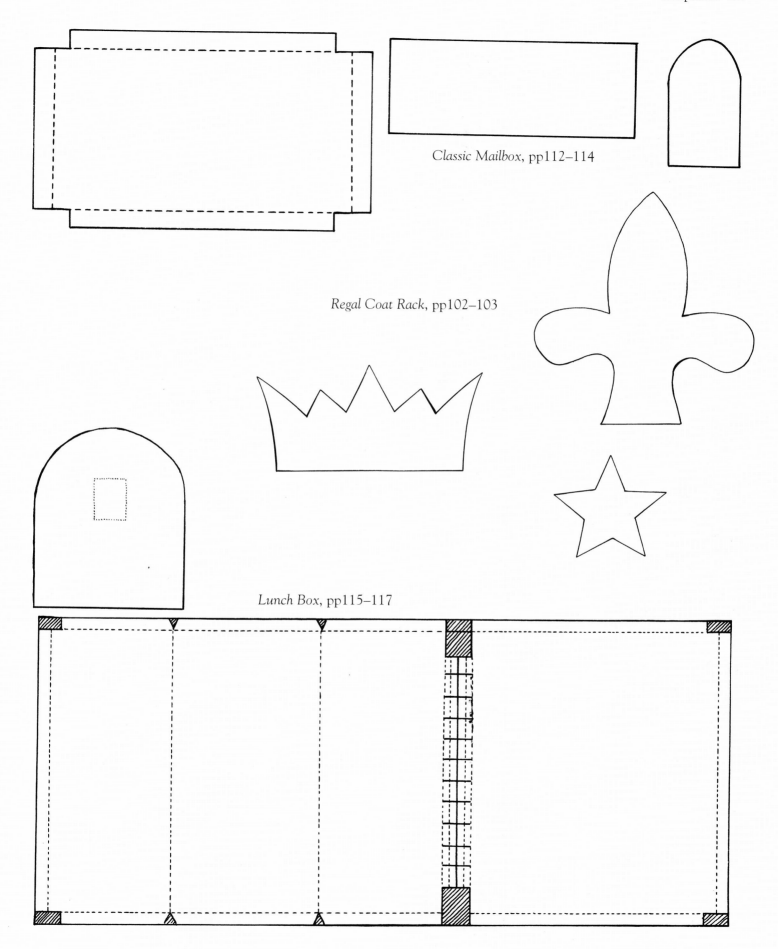

Classic Mailbox, pp112–114

Regal Coat Rack, pp102–103

Lunch Box, pp115–117

Index